Complete Starter Guide to
Whittling

FOX CHAPEL
PUBLISHING

Complete Starter Guide to
Whittling

© 2013 by Fox Chapel Publishing Company, Inc., 903 Square Street, Mount Joy, PA 17552.
Complete Starter Guide to Whittling is an original work, first published in 2013 by Fox Chapel Publishing Company, Inc. The patterns contained herein are copyrighted by the authors. Readers may make copies of these patterns for personal use. The patterns themselves, however, are not to be duplicated for resale or distribution under any circumstances. Any such copying is a violation of copyright law.

ISBN 978-1-56523-842-8

To learn more about the other great books from Fox Chapel Publishing, or to find a retailer near you, call toll-free 800-457-9112 or visit us at *www.FoxChapelPublishing.com*.

We are always looking for talented authors. To submit an idea, please send a brief inquiry to acquisitions@foxchapelpublishing.com.

Printed in Singapore
Twelfth printing

ON THE WEB
www.woodcarvingillustrated.com

➤ *Amazing Chain Gallery*
Hand-Carved Classics, pg. 36
Challenge yourself to create intricate chains and cages.

➤ *Safety Tips for Kids*
Flying Propeller, pg. 17
Rick Wiebe shares time-tested tips for teaching kids.

➤ *Bonus Instructions*
Whittling a Decorative Fishing Lure, pg. 70
Follow Lora Irish's instructions to make a copper-wire display stand for your lure.

Choosing a
Whittling
Knife

What to look for when selecting a folding knife

By Bob Duncan

One of the neat things about whittling is that you can do it anywhere. This means your knife should be portable, and nothing beats the convenience of safely slipping a folded knife into your pocket.

Many manufacturers create folding knives for whittling (or carving) with blades that resemble classic carving knives. These specialty knives can get expensive, and are worth the money if you do a lot of whittling, but you don't need to buy a specialty knife to whittle.

Many carvers use a second pocketknife for everyday use, such as opening cardboard boxes, to avoid dulling the sharp pocketknife they use for whittling.

When selecting a pocketknife for whittling, there are a few things to keep in mind.

Carbon Steel Blade

Many pocketknife blades are made from stainless steel. Most carving tools are made from high-carbon steel. Stainless steel holds an edge for a long time and doesn't corrode if you close the knife with a wet blade—both great qualities for pocketknives. But because stainless steel dulls slowly, it sharpens slowly as well. Knives with high-carbon steel blades are more expensive than knives with stainless steel blades, but they are easier to sharpen.

Many manufacturers are creating high-carbon stainless steel blades, which combine the durability of stainless steel with the added benefits of carbon steel.

Blade Location

Some pocketknives have ten to twenty blades. These knives are generally less comfortable to use for long periods of time, and the blades you want to carve with are seldom in the center of the handle. If the knife blade is not in the center of the handle, you lose leverage, which reduces your carving power and control. Instead, look for a knife with two or, at most, three blades, which should ensure the blades are conveniently placed.

Blade Shape

Look for a sheepsfoot blade—one where the tip of the knife is closely aligned with the main cutting edge, similar to a utility knife or standard bench knife. Many pocketknife blades have a drop-point shape, which centers the tip

A sheepsfoot blade (top) is better suited for whittling than a drop-point blade (bottom).

of the knife in the middle of the blade. The drop-point shape works well for general cutting purposes, but makes it difficult to carve small details. You can reshape a blade using sharpening stones and sandpaper, but the process is time consuming (see page 23).

Locking Blades

A locking blade keeps the sharp knife from accidentally closing on your fingers, which is a good safety feature. However, as long as you are always aware a knife can close on your fingers, you should be safe, regardless of whether or not your knife features a locking blade.

Choosing the Right Knife for You

Selecting the ideal pocketknife for you is a matter of personal preference. The size of your grip compared with the size of the handle will greatly influence how comfortable the knife is to use over extended periods. The ideal knife for your friend may not be well-suited for you. Ask other whittlers for their opinions and if possible, handle several knives before making a purchase.

LESS THAN $50

Folding Utility Knife (around $10)
Available at most home stores
Pros:
- Inexpensive
- Replaceable blades eliminate the need to sharpen

Cons:
- The large triangular blade can be difficult to control in tight areas
- Requires inventory of replacement blades
- Blade can break if you pry with the blade or apply force to the sides of the blade

Woodcraft Two-Blade Folding Carving Knife ($20)
Available through Woodcraft, 800-225-1153, www.woodcraft.com
Pros:
- High-carbon stainless steel blades
- Two blade shapes, including a chip carving blade
- Ergonomical wood inlay handle
- Small detail blade fits into tight areas

Cons:
- Short blades make carving larger projects difficult
- Blades do not lock open

Buck Trio ($26)
Contact Buck Knives to find a local dealer, 800-326-2825, www.buckknives.com
Pros:
- Three blade shapes allow you to carve different areas
- Large blade for fast stock removal
- Sheepsfoot blade for general carving
- Pointed pen blade for detail carving

Cons:
- Stainless steel blades
- Blades do not lock open

Victorinox Swiss Army Tinker ($26)
Contact Victorinox Swiss Army to find a local dealer, 800-422-2706, www.swissarmy.com
Pros:
- Two blades
- Small detail blade fits into tight areas
- Large blade for fast stock removal

Cons:
- Stainless steel blades
- Blades do not lock open
- Includes extra tools not used for carving
- Must remove key ring for comfortable carving

Woodcraft Double-Blade Long Handle Carving Knife ($26)

Available through Woodcraft, 800-225-1153, www.woodcraft.com

Pros:
- High-carbon stainless steel blades
- Two blade shapes, including a chip carving blade
- Ergonomical wood inlay handle
- Large blade for fast stock removal

Cons:
- Long blades make carving tight areas difficult
- Blades do not lock open

Case Stockman ($36)

Contact W. R. Case and Sons to find a local dealer, 800-523-6350, www.wrcase.com

Pros:
- Three blade shapes allow you to carve different areas
- Large blade for fast stock removal
- Sheepsfoot blade for general carving
- Pointed pen blade for detail carving
- Made in USA

Cons:
- Stainless steel blades
- Blades do not lock open

Buck Stockman ($30)

Contact Buck Knives to find a local dealer, 800-326-2825, www.buckknives.com

Pros:
- Three blade shapes allow you to carve different areas
- Large blade for fast stock removal
- Sheepsfoot blade for general carving
- Pointed pen blade for detail carving

Cons:
- Stainless steel blades
- Blades do not lock open
- Slightly larger than Buck Trio, so it can be more difficult to carve details

Case Seahorse Whittler ($45)

The Seahorse Whittler was just discontinued so supplies are limited, but this is one of the most popular whittling knives. Some online retailers still have the knife in stock.

Pros:
- Large blade for fast stock removal
- Small sheepsfoot and pointed pen blades for detail carving
- Made in USA

Cons:
- Stainless steel blades
- Blades do not lock open

$50 OR MORE

Buck Lancer ($50)

Contact Buck Knives to find a local dealer, 800-326-2825, www.buckknives.com

Pros:
- Smallest two-blade knife Buck makes
- Large blade for fast stock removal
- Sheepsfoot blade for general carving
- High-carbon steel blades
- Made in USA

Cons:
- Blades do not lock open

Case Whittler ($50)

Contact W. R. Case and Sons to find a local dealer, 800-523-6350, www.wrcase.com

Pros:
- Large blade for fast stock removal
- Small detail blades fits into tight areas
- Made in USA

Cons:
- Stainless steel blades
- Blades do not lock open

Flexcut Whittling Jack ($50)

Available from Flexcut, 800-524-9077,
www.flexcut.com

Pros:
- Tempered spring steel holds and
  edge and sharpens easily
- Includes a roughing-out blade and a detail blade
- Made in the USA
- Comfortable wood and metal handle
- Lightweight tool fits easily in a pocket

Cons:
- Blades do not lock

Kershaw Double Cross ($55, $58 if modified for carving)

Available from several suppliers, but knives
modified for easier carving by Little Shavers
(206-767-7421, www.littleshavers.com) are
popular among carvers.

Pros
- Large blade for fast stock removal
- Small detail blade fits into tight areas
- Locking blades
- Stainless steel alloy is easy to sharpen and resists staining

Cons
- Stainless steel alloy doesn't hold an edge as long
  as other stainless steel

Oar Carver Single Lockers ($65)

Available from Stadtlander Woodcarving,
585-593-6911, www.stadtlandercarvings.com

Pros:
- High-carbon steel blade
- Large blade for fast stock removal
- Tapered blade shape allows detail carving
- Locking blade
- Made in USA

Cons:
- Single blade limits ability to carve small details

Flexcut Pocket Jack ($80)

Available from Flexcut, 800-524-9077,
www.flexcut.com

Pros:
- Tempered spring steel holds an edge and sharpens easily
- Combines a detail knife with a straight gouge,
  scorp, and V-scorp
- Locking blades
- Made in USA

Cons:
- Takes time to get used to shape of handle
  with additional tools

Oar Carver Version II ($70)

Available from Stadtlander Woodcarving,
585-593-6911, www.stadtlandercarvings.com

Pros:
- High-carbon steel blades
- Small detail blade fits into tight areas
- Large blade for fast stock removal
- Made in USA

Cons:
- Blades do not lock open

Flexcut Carvin' Jack ($136)

Available from Flexcut, 800-524-9077,
www.flexcut.com

Pros:
- Tempered spring steel holds an edge and sharpens easily
- Right- and left-handed versions available for
  additional comfort
- Features a detail knife, bent knife, straight chisel, gouge,
  scorp, and V-scorp
- Locking blades
- Made in USA

Cons:
- Additional tools make the handle a bit bulky and
  uncomfortable for long carving sessions

Whittling Safety & Basic Knife Cuts

By Bob Duncan

A few simple rules prevent injuries when whittling

There is risk involved whenever you handle sharp tools. A knife sharp enough to cut through wood will easily cut skin. Most cuts are small nicks that heal quickly and don't leave a scar. However, it's best to follow simple safety procedures to prevent serious injuries.

The fundamental rule when it comes to whittling is to be aware not only of where the blade is, but where the blade could go. Wood can change density at any point, and you need to change the amount of pressure you apply on the knife based on the wood density. Imagine pushing hard to cut through a hard knot only to find a softer section of wood behind the knot. The sharp edge will quickly slice through the softer area and cut into whatever is on the other side. The knife doesn't care if it's open air, a carving bench, or your hand.

Wear a glove on the hand holding your carving.

Boy Scouts are taught to always cut away from themselves. While this is good advice, there are times when you cut toward your thumb, such as when making a paring cut (see page 10). When making a paring cut, wear a leather thumb protector, wrap your thumb with cloth tape, or position your thumb far enough down on the project so if the knife slips, it won't hit your thumb.

Because most cuts occur on the hand holding the project, carvers often wear a cut-resistant glove on that hand. It is possible to prevent cuts by being aware of where the sharp edge can (and

Wear a thumb guard when cutting toward your thumb.

probably will) go. Always cut away from yourself when you are removing bark or large amounts of wood. When you are carving finer details, anchor your holding hand to the carving hand. Place the thumb of your holding hand on the back of the thumb on the knife-holding hand when doing a push cut. Or, rest the fingers of your knife hand on the fingers of your holding hand. Anchoring your hands adds stability and control, making it less likely that the knife will slip.

Cut away from yourself to prevent injury.

Some whittlers use their thighs as carving benches. A cut on your thigh can be serious. Carving on a workbench or table is recommended. If you cut toward your thigh, invest in a strip of leather to protect your leg.

Without proper precautions, a slip of the knife can result in an emergency-room visit. Follow these simple safety rules and you'll never require anything more than a Band-aid.

Complete most projects with four types of cuts

Like most types of carving (woodcarving, ice carving, stone carving), whittling is a subtractive art—you remove all of the material that isn't part of your vision for the final piece. For example, to carve a dog, remove all of the wood that doesn't contribute to the shape of the dog.

Most whittlers use four basic cuts to remove excess wood: the push cut, the paring cut, the stop cut, and the V-shaped cut. Master these four basic types of cuts and you'll be ready to tackle a multitude of projects.

PUSH CUT

For the push cut, hold the wood in one hand. Hold the knife in your other hand with the thumb on the back of the blade. Push the knife through the wood, away from your body. This type of cut is also called the straightaway cut. For additional control or power, place the thumb of the wood-holding hand on top of the thumb on the blade, and use the wood-holding thumb as a pivot as you rotate the wrist of your knife-holding hand. This maneuver is often called the thumb-pushing cut or lever cut.

The paring cut gives you a great deal of control but requires you to cut toward your thumb. Wear a thumb protector or be aware of where the knife could cut at all times, especially if it slips beyond the anticipated stopping point. To perform the paring cut, which is also called the draw cut, hold the wood in one hand. Hold the knife in the other hand with four fingers. The cutting edge points toward your thumb. Rest the thumb of your knife-holding hand on the wood behind the area you want to carve. Extend the thumb as much as possible. Close your hand, pulling the knife toward your thumb, to slice through the wood. This is the same action used to peel (or pare) potatoes.

PARING CUT

As the name suggests, the stop cut is used to create a hard line at the end of another cut. Your hand position depends on the placement of the cut you need to make. Regardless of your hand position, simply cut straight into the wood to create a stop cut. Make a stop cut first to prevent a consecutive cut from extending beyond the intended area. Make a stop cut second to free a chip of wood remaining from a primary cut.

STOP CUT

To make a V-shaped cut, hold a knife the same way you do when making a paring cut. Anchor the thumb of the knife hand against the wood and cut in at an angle with the tip of the knife. Rotate the wood, anchor your thumb on the other side of the cut, and cut in at an angle, running beside the first cut. Angle the two cuts so the bottom or deepest part of the cuts meet in the center. This creates a V-shaped groove. Use the center of the cutting edge to make intersecting angled cuts on the corner of a blank, creating V-shaped notches.

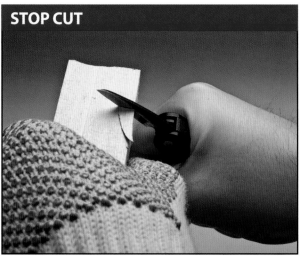

V-SHAPED CUT

The Basics of
Sharpening

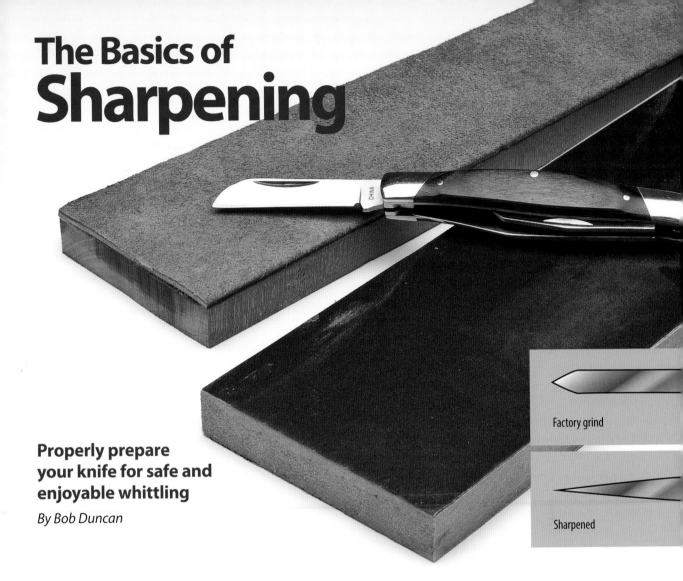

Factory grind

Sharpened

Properly prepare your knife for safe and enjoyable whittling

By Bob Duncan

Although it may seem contradictory, a sharp knife is a safe knife. When a knife is dull, or not shaped properly, it requires more force to push the blade through the wood. The more force required to make the cut, the less control you have. Because a sharp, properly shaped blade requires less force, it reduces fatigue, resulting in a more enjoyable carving experience. Many novice carvers get discouraged because they are carving with a dull knife or a blade that is not shaped properly.

Sharpening is a simple process, but it takes practice to execute successfully. If you boil it down to the basics, sharpening consists of rubbing a piece of metal against an abrasive to create a wedge shape. It takes practice to consistently hold the metal against the abrasive at the correct angle.

When it comes to choosing an abrasive to sharpen with, you can use anything from simple sandpaper to elaborate power sharpeners. With any method, the basic process is the same—use a coarse abrasive to wear away the metal of the blade until the blade is the shape you want. Then, use progressively finer grits of abrasive to remove the scratches from the previous grit until you have a polished edge.

Manufacturers seldom shape the blade of their pocketknives with carvers in mind. Typically, the factory edge consists of a gradual bevel on the blade that becomes a steep wedge at the cutting edge. This type of edge is durable, and works well for cutting rope and cardboard boxes, but you need a flatter bevel for carving wood.

There are many methods and products to help you achieve a sharp cutting edge, but I recommend beginners start with sandpaper. Use spray adhesive to attach 6" (152mm)-long strips of sandpaper to a perfectly flat surface, such as glass or medium-density fiberboard (MDF). For the initial bevel shaping, start with 200- to 320-grit wet/dry sandpaper. Wet/dry sandpaper is more durable than regular sandpaper. Work your way up through the grits to 600 grit, and then polish the blade on a leather strop.

SHARPENING A BLADE

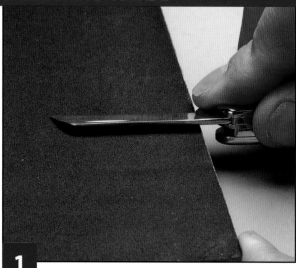

1 **Begin shaping the bevel.** Hold the entire length of the blade flat against 200- or 320-grit sandpaper with the cutting edge facing away from you. Lift the back of the blade slightly (about 1/32" or 1mm). Maintain the same angle as you push the knife away from you, toward the cutting edge, and along the length of the sandpaper.

2 **Shape the other side of the blade.** Lift the blade off the sandpaper and flip the knife over so the cutting edge is facing toward you. Lay the entire length of the blade on the sandpaper and lift the back slightly (1/32" or 1mm). Pull the blade toward the cutting edge, along the length of the sandpaper, maintaining a consistent angle.

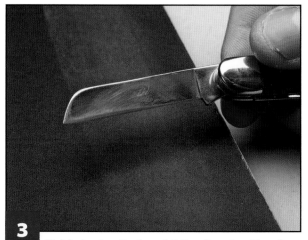

3 **Finish shaping the bevel.** Follow Steps 1 and 2 until you create the desired bevel across the length of the blade. You should see shiny metal where you've removed the old bevel and reshaped the blade.

4 **Remove the scratches from the coarser sandpaper.** Repeat Steps 1 through 3 as you work through 400-grit and then 600-grit sandpaper. Remove the visible scratches from the coarser sandpaper before moving to the next finer grit.

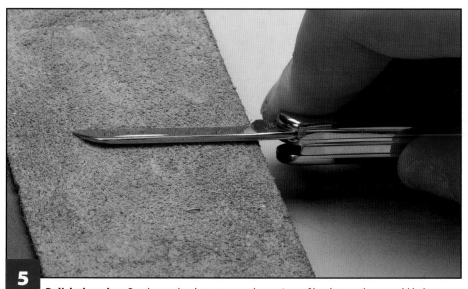

5 **Polish the edge.** Purchase a leather strop or glue a piece of leather, such as an old belt, to a flat piece of wood with the rough side facing up. Apply a small amount of stropping compound to the leather. Stropping compound is available in powder form at hardware and auto parts stores. The grit is not important for stropping carving knives. Position the entire length of the blade on the leather strop and lift the back of the blade slightly (1/32" or 1mm). Draw the blade across the strop, moving away from the cutting edge. Do not push the blade toward the cutting edge or you will damage the strop and round the cutting edge. At the end of the strop, lift the blade, flip the knife over, and place the other side flat on the strop. Lift the back of the blade slightly (1/32" or 1mm) and draw the blade along the strop, moving away from the cutting edge. This process polishes the blade for a cleaner and smoother cut. Once the bevel has been shaped, maintain the cutting edge by stropping often. You only need to sharpen with sandpaper if you nick the blade or damage the cutting edge.

Quick Carve Spreader

Carve this useful utensil out of a branch using only a pocketknife

By Chris Lubkemann

This simple spreader makes a thoughtful gift when paired with homemade jam. The spreader is just a wooden knife with a blunt tip. It's easy to carve from a short straight knot-free branch. I usually carve green wood—that's just my style. You can easily find it when camping or hiking, or even in your backyard.

If the branch you find has a slight curve, make sure when you carve the blade, you end up with a blade that is straight when you look at it from the top. Seeing the curve of the branch from the side is fine. If there is any knot on the branch, it should be either at the butt end of the handle or at the spot where the handle transitions to the blade.

Once you've mastered the spreader, use the same technique to make variations such as a letter opener (see page 76), a knife, a tapered skewer for cooking hotdogs, a toasting fork, or a spoon.

See page 9 for basic carving instructions.

SPREADER: FORMING THE HANDLE

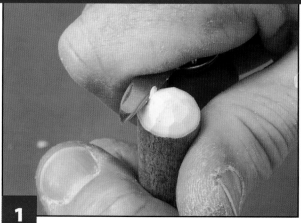

1 **Choose a blank.** I've chosen a maple branch about ¾" (19mm) diameter and 8" (203mm) long. Use the draw cutting stroke to round the butt of the handle.

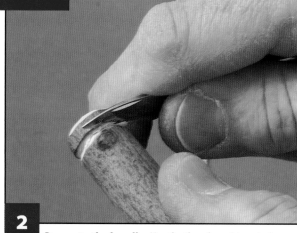

2 **Decorate the handle.** Use the thumb pushing stroke to cut a V-shaped groove around the end of the handle. Then, cut another groove farther down the handle. Locate this groove just a bit above where you want the blade of the spreader to start. Again, use the thumb push stroke.

SPREADER: CARVING THE BLADE

3 **Flatten the blade.** Use long straight strokes to flatten the blade on both sides.

4 **Narrow the neck.** Continue carving until the blade is centered on the handle. Then, narrow the neck of the spreader. Use both pushing and drawing cuts—always cutting toward the center—to narrow the part between the handle and the blade.

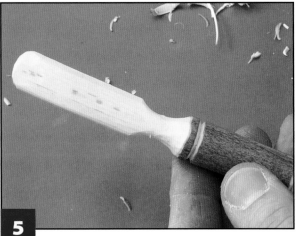

5 **Round the end.** Carve a curved tip and continue shaping the blade until you're satisfied.

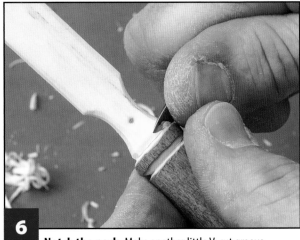

6 **Notch the neck.** Make another little V-cut groove between the neck and the handle.

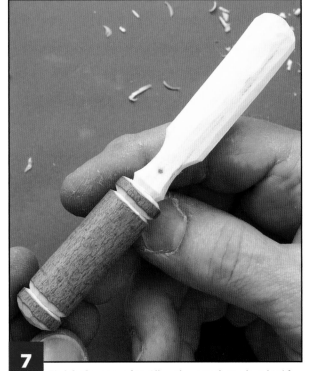

7 **Finish the spreader.** Allow the spreader to dry a bit (if you used green wood). Then, give it a final sanding. Apply a clear food-safe finish of your choice (optional).

For more information on Chris Lubkemann, see page 96.

For more information on Chris Lubkemann, see page 96.

further reading

Tree Craft
by Chris Lubkemann

If you're creative, have an appreciation for wood, and can work with a few basic tools, you can create the thirty-five unique and practical projects in Tree Craft. *Bringing the natural elegance of the outdoors into your home is easier than you think. Learn how to transform twigs, branches, and fallen trees into artfully designed candle holders, coat racks, coffee tables, and more to flavor your home with an eco-chic style.*

Available for $19.95 from Fox Chapel Publishing, 1970 Broad St., East Petersburg, Pa., 17520, 800-457-9112, www.foxchapelpublishing.com, or check your local retailer.

materials & tools

MATERIALS:
- ¾"-diameter x 8"-long (19mm x 203mm) green branch
- Fine-grit sandpaper
- Clear finish (optional)
- Pencil (optional)
- Cyanoacrylate (CA) glue (optional)

TOOLS:
- Carving knife
- Woodburner (optional)

The author used these products for the project. Substitute your choice of brands, tools, and materials as desired.

Flying Propeller

Classic toy anyone can make

By Rick Wiebe

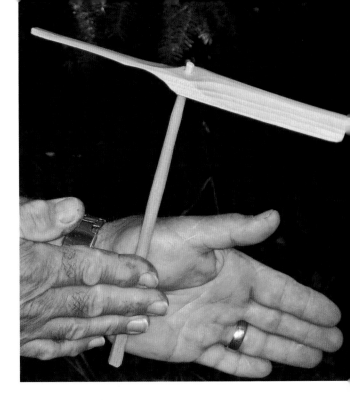

This simple project doesn't take long to finish and kids can play with it as soon as it's complete. I use white pine, but other soft woods, such as ponderosa pine, spruce, or basswood, will also work well. Avoid using really hard woods or woods that split easily.

To fly the propeller, hold the bottom of the handle against the heel of your left hand with the fingers of your right hand. Reverse the hands for a left-handed propeller. Push the right hand forward, keeping your thumbs out of the way, while applying pressure to the handle. If the propeller smacks you in the hands, spin the propeller the other way.

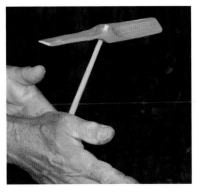

PROPELLER: PREPARING THE BLANK

1 **Square the edges of the blank.** Carve the stick down to 5⁄16" by 1" by 8" (8mm by 25mm by 203mm). The blank must be a consistent thickness and width with sharp 90° corners. Mark the location of the hole for the handle by measuring 4" (102mm) from one end and making a mark ½" (13mm) in from the edge.

2 **Drill the hole for the handle.** Use a ¼" (6mm)-diameter drill bit or one of the drilling blades on a specialty pocketknife. Do not try to drill the hole with a normal knife blade; this will split the wood, dull your knife, create a fuzzy hole, or cause an injury.

PROPELLER: SHAPING THE BLADES

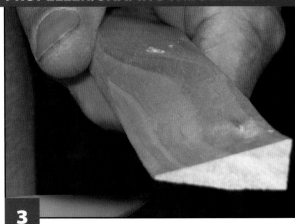

3 **Whittle off the right corner of the blank.** Start about ¼" (6mm) from the hole. If you are left handed, whittle off the left corner of the blank and make a left-handed propeller. Do not carve away the bottom edge. Turn the blank end to end and repeat on the opposite end. Make the ends as much like each other as possible.

4 **Thin the propellers.** Flip the blank and whittle off wood to make the propeller as thin as possible. Follow the profiles you carved in Step 3. Do not cut through the edges.

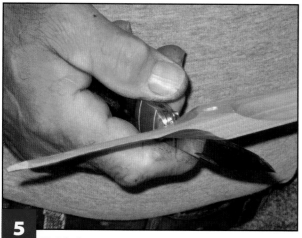

5 **Finish the propeller.** Round the sharp corners. To balance the propeller, line the edge of the blade up on the center of the hole and see if the propeller tips. If so, shave wood off of the heavy side a little at a time until the propeller teeters equally in both directions. Do not shave off too much wood.

6 **Cut the handle.** The handle blank should be about 1" (25mm) longer than the propeller. This stabilizes the propeller and helps it fly, even if the balance isn't perfect. If you have trouble flying the propeller, make a slightly longer handle.

7 **Shape the handle.** Carve the handle blank down to the diameter of a fat pencil with a long tapered end that fits snugly into the hole in the propeller. If the handle doesn't fit tightly, glue it in place.

For more information on Rick Wiebe, see page 96.

materials & tools

MATERIALS:
- ½" x 1½" x 8" (13mm x 38mm x 203mm) white pine, ponderosa pine, or basswood (propeller)
- ½" x ½" x 9" (13mm x 13mm x 229mm) white pine, ponderosa pine, or basswood (handle)
- Wood glue (optional)

TOOLS:
- Pocketknife
- Drill with ¼" (6mm)-diameter bit (or knife with a special drilling blade)

The author used these products for the project. Substitute your choice of brands, tools, and materials as desired.

Whittle a
Twig Whistle

New technique reinvents a perennial favorite

by Chris Lubkemann

As I've traveled around the country, I can't even begin to tell you the number of folks who have told me that they used to make whistles from tree branches. Their whistles tend to be the "tap-the-bark/slide-it-off/notch-the-wood/slide-the-bark-back-on/and-blow" variety. Of course, only certain woods work with that technique, and generally whistle manufacturing has to be done in the spring when the sap is running and the wood is very wet.

These instructions are for a simple but fun whistle you can make from a couple of round pieces of dry branch (or even a broom handle) any time of year!

1 **Drill a hole.** Clamp the thicker branch in a vise. Drill a hole lengthwise through the branch, stopping before you get to the end.

2 **Strip the bark.** At the hole end of the whistle, remove 1" (25mm)-long strips of bark halfway around the branch.

3 **Smooth the end.** Round and smooth the mouthpiece.

4 **Carve a notch.** Notch the barked side of the branch with repeated straight and diagonal cuts until the cut extends about halfway through the drilled hole.

5 **Choose a second branch.** Select a smaller branch that has a diameter slightly greater than the diameter of the hole.

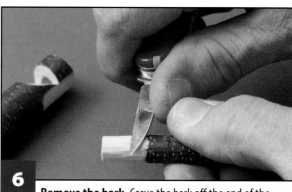

6 **Remove the bark.** Carve the bark off the end of the smaller branch, leaving about ¾" (19mm) bare.

7 **Shape the branch.** Round the carved end of the smaller branch and flatten one side.

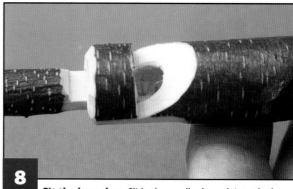

8 **Fit the branches.** Slide the smaller branch into the larger one with the flat side up until it just reaches the edge of the notch.

9 **Trim the branch.** Cut the thin branch flush with the mouthpiece of the whistle.

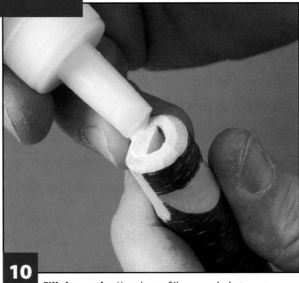

10 **Fill the cracks.** Use glue to fill any cracks between the large and small twigs. Let the glue dry, and then try the whistle. If the hole is "clean as a whistle," it should work. If the whistle doesn't work, wait until the wood dries further and then your whistle should sound.

materials & tools

MATERIALS:
- 2 pieces of straight-grained, well-dried wood, one thicker than the other
- Glue

TOOLS:
- Vise
- Knife
- Drill with bit to fit inside larger branch

The author used these products for the project. Substitute your choice of brands, tools, and materials as desired.

further reading

The Little Book of Whittling
by Chris Lubkemann

Author Chris Lubkemann will help you whittle away the hours with clear guidance on becoming an expert whittler. Whether you're a beginner looking for an easy way to get started in the most basic form of woodcarving or an advanced carver looking for a relaxing way to spend your free time, The Little Book of Whittling *will give you the how-to instruction you need to become an accomplished whittler.*

Available for $12.95 from Fox Chapel Publishing, 1970 Broad St., East Petersburg, Pa., 17520, www.foxchapelpublishing.com, 800-457-9112, or check your local retailer.

For more information on Chris Lubkemann, see page 96.

Making a Grass Whistle
Remember whistling with a blade of grass when you were little? Most of us have forgotten how to do it. Here's a reminder:

1. *Find a blade of grass approximately ¼" (6mm) wide.*
2. *Hold your thumbs together so your nails are facing you.*
3. *Sandwich the blade of grass between your thumbs. Create a smooth, straight fit.*
4. *Place your lips over the opening between your thumbs and blow! Experiment with harder and softer blows for different sounds.*

Altering a Pocketknife to
Whittle Twigs & Curls

Specific alterations are needed to the shape of a knife blade if you want to carve perfect curls from a tree branch.

On the Tinker, I file off the key ring and tab to make the handle more comfortable. File off any sharp edges or corners.

TAPER THE SMALL BLADE

The drop-point shape of the blade makes it difficult to make small cuts in tight spaces. I use coarse sandpaper or a file to shape the tip of the small blade on the Tinker. I remove the wedge and give it a flat bevel while sharpening (see page 11).

Properly prepare a pocketknife for whittling twigs and branches

By Chris Lubkemann

I carve most of my pieces using a simple two-blade pocketknife. I suggest a Victorinox Swiss Army Tinker for people interested in carving twigs and branches like I do.

Out of the box, most pocketknives, the Tinker included, will not work to carve curls. The factory grind on the blade, which works well for general cutting tasks, is too wedge-shaped for carving. However, simple alterations will have you carving beautiful curls in no time.

Most pocketknives have a drop-point-shaped blade, where the cutting edge is straight over most of its length, but curves up sharply at the tip, which is centered in the middle of the blade. I find a blade that is tapered to the tip, rather than curved, allows me to make more accurate small radius cuts.

In order to carve little things in twigs and branches, I modify my pocketknives. On the Tinker, I taper the smaller blade to make it easier to cut in small areas. I change the shape of the bevel on the larger blade slightly and use this blade to cut curls, such as the petals on my flowers (see page 24).

SHAPE THE LARGE BLADE

The wedge-shaped factory edge on most pocketknives doesn't work well for carving.

Sharpen the blade to conform to the illustration above.

On the large blade of the Tinker, I carefully round over the shoulders, removing the wedge shape of the blade.

Whittling a
Flower

by Chris Lubkemann

Over the years, I've whittled thousands of little flowers, the majority just given to folks along the way. I used to throw little scraps away until I discovered that just about every single one of them could be turned into a flower, complete with petals, stem, and leaves.

Carving this type of flower is really not that uncommon. Many people do it. I'll just share my own take on a quick and fun little project, one that can be expanded upon and applied very widely.

Most of the flowers of this type that I've seen are quite a bit larger than the ones I make. Usually the flower itself is made and cut off; then, a stem of some kind is inserted in a little hole that is drilled in the base of the flower. My own flowers are all made from one continuous piece of wood, usually a thin, close-grained twig or branch. The branches I use are relatively straight, don't have many knots, and generally are from ¹⁄₁₆ inch to ¼ inch in diameter. Because moisture really affects the petals in this project, be sure to find wood that is between freshly cut and completely dry. A freshly cut branch that is de-barked will dry nicely in a relatively short time, maybe even in a few hours.

1 Eight little starting blanks. I'm guessing that these branches could result in 18 to 20 flowers, complete with stems and leaves.

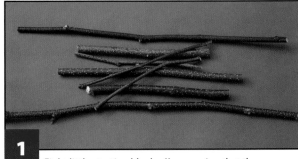

2 Using long, straight strokes, remove the bark from the branch. (Some carvers prefer to leave the bark on the branch in order to give the outside ring of petals a different look. If you decide to do this, make sure the wood you're using has tight bark that won't just fall off after the flower dries out.)

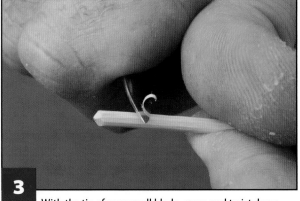

3 With the tip of your small blade, carve and twist down the first layer of petals, cutting all the way around the branch, always cutting down to the same depth.

4 Carve down another layer or two. Try to position the second layer of petals between the petals of the previously carved layer.

5 Twist out the little central core that's left in the middle.

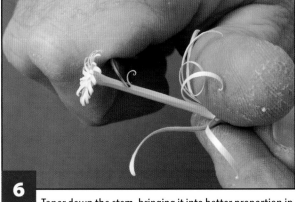

6 Taper down the stem, bringing it into better proportion in relation to the size of the flower. (Of course you can always leave the stem thick. Then you have a little palm tree!)

7 Carve down a couple more little shavings to serve as the leaves.

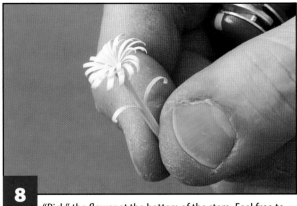

8 "Pick" the flower at the bottom of the stem. Feel free to move the petals around a bit and position them where you want. They're really very sturdy and forgiving. Now the flower is ready for finishing: painting, mounting, "planting," and whatever else you choose. I've found that chunks of bark or thick mulch serve nicely as natural bases.

Jumping
Fish

by Chris Lubkemann

Transform a small branch

Fish of all kinds are another specialty of many woodcarvers. When I attend carving shows, I'm totally amazed at the incredible lifelikeness and detail of the fish I see. If we dropped some of these carvings in a large aquarium, we'd never know we weren't observing live fish! The fish that follows is definitely not intended to fall into the same category as the earlier-mentioned works of art. However, I think you'll enjoy carving it. I know I did.

For this project, I'm indebted to fellow branch carver Mike Shatt of Milford, Pennsylvania. Quite a few years back, I met Mike and introduced him to the concept of carving twigs and branches. Several years ago, Mike sent me a few photos of pieces he had carved. Among them were several of fish jumping out of water, complete with splash! Based on his idea, I tried similar fish myself. If you don't have a branch with another little branch growing from the side to make the fish's dorsal fin, you can use a separate branch for the dorsal fin.

1 If you can, start with a blank branch that has better built-in potential for a good dorsal fin. Start by making a little sketch.

materials
& tools

MATERIALS:
• Forked branch of choice

TOOLS:
• Knife
• Sandpaper—a couple of grits on the fine to very fine side (150- and 220-grit would work).
• Pencil, pen, or marker.

The author used these products for the project.
Substitute your choice of brands, tools, and materials as desired.

2 Remove all of the bark from the entire branch.

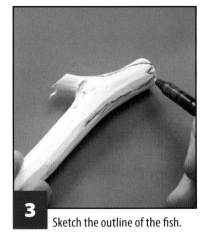

3 Sketch the outline of the fish.

4 Remove wood from outside the lines.

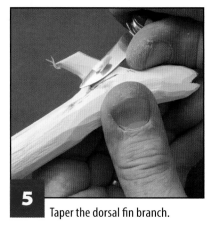

5 Taper the dorsal fin branch.

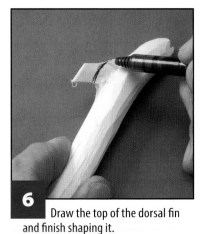

6 Draw the top of the dorsal fin and finish shaping it.

7 Sand the whole fish smooth.

8 With the tip of your small blade, drawcut little shavings all the way around the fish. These little shavings and curls will constitute the upward-splashing water.

9 Make four little forward cuts to add the fish's other little fins. What you'll be doing is just lifting a little shaving to serve as a fin.

10 Cut the wood just below the splash and mount it on a cross-grained slice of wood with the growth rings clearly visible. The rings sort of give the effect of ripples radiating out from the splash.

Santa Pencils

Turn ordinary pencils into festive Santas in eight simple steps

By Ron Johnson
Step-by-step photos by James A. Johnson

This quick-carve project is lots of fun and makes a perfect stocking stuffer. Santa's face is carved into an ordinary pencil, an affordable material which is readily found at dollar stores and discount stores.

My first exposure to carving pencils was in 2002 when a local carver named Elmer Sellers showed me how to carve a face in a standard pencil using only a knife. Since then, my carving technique has evolved, and I have given away hundreds of Santa pencils over the years.

Leave a Santa pencil with a tip at restaurants or give them to anyone who shows an interest. Carving pencils at a picnic table in a campground always brings interested visitors. The Santa pencils are a traditional Christmas treat for my granddaughter's teacher and classmates. Cut off the lower portion of the pencil and thread a string through the eraser for a unique Christmas ornament.

Carve printed pencils on the side opposite the printing or carve away the printing when you remove the paint. A good material source is a local supplier that imprints pencils for advertising. Buy the pencils without printing in your color of choice.

I use red hexagonal pencils to instantly convey Santa's red suit. Round pencils work just as well, but I suggest you use a hexagonal pencil for your first attempt. Use plain wooden pencils and leave them unpainted to represent wood spirits. You can also carve flat carpenter's pencils.

1 **Shape the forehead.** Use the ridge between two flat planes of the pencil as a centerline. Make a stop cut perpendicular to the ridge ½" (13mm) down from the metal collar and as deep as the two adjacent ridges. Do not cut deep enough to hit pencil lead. Move down ³⁄₁₆" (5mm) and cut up to the stop cut to remove a V-shaped chip.

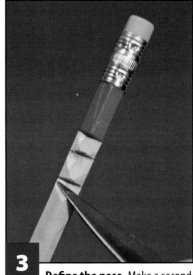

2 **Remove the paint from the carving area.** Start about 2" (51mm) below the stop cut made in Step 1. Hold your knife at a low angle and slice the paint off the flat planes on either side of the centerline. It may take four or more slices to remove the paint. If your knife digs into the grain, start your cut from the other end.

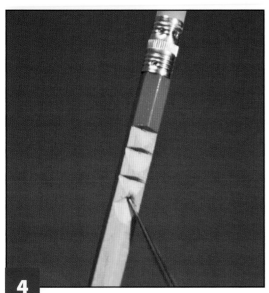

3 **Define the nose.** Make a second stop cut just below the start of the angled cut made in Step 1. Move down ³⁄₁₆" (5mm) and cut up to the stop cut to remove the chip. Move down ¼" (6mm) from the second stop cut and make a third stop cut. Carve up to the third stop cut from ³⁄₁₆" (5mm) below to remove a third chip.

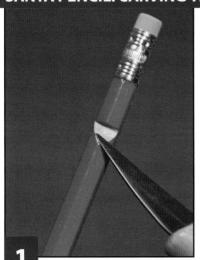

Define the mustache. Move down an additional ³⁄₁₆" (5mm) and position the knife point on the centerline ridge. Make a cut at a 45° angle from the centerline down to the edge of the flat plane. Repeat for the other side of the mustache. Cut up from ³⁄₁₆" (5mm) below the center of the mustache to remove the chip. Remove the centerline ridge from the mustache down to the painted area.

TIPS SAFE CARVING

Choose full-size pencils and hold the lower portion, well below the carving area, in your non-carving hand. Hold the upper part of the pencil on a flat hard surface for controlled safe cuts.

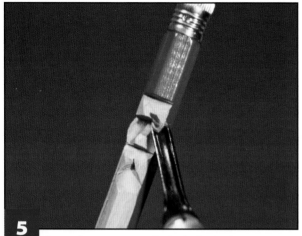

5 **Carve the nose.** Vertically divide the third stop cut, just above the mustache, into thirds. Carve away the two outer thirds with a ⅛" (3mm) #11 gouge. Angle the cuts toward the centerline slightly. Leave the center third as the nose. Varying the angle of these gouge cuts increases or decreases the width of the nose. Use a knife to free the chips if necessary.

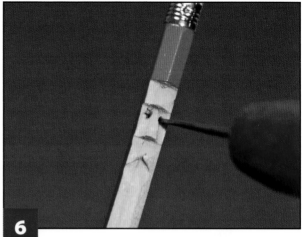

6 **Carve the eyes.** Stab the point of an old knife straight down, perpendicular to the pencil, at the top of the gouge cut made in Step 5. Move it back and forth a few times to create the eye. Repeat the process for the other eye. Position the back side of the knife toward the nose to make symmetrical eyes.

SANTA PENCIL: ADDING THE DETAILS

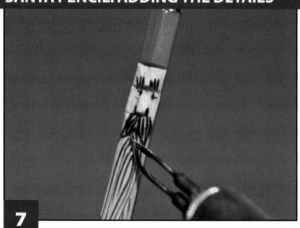

7 **Create the texture and shadows.** You can carve the texture before burning or create the texture using only a woodbuner. Add three short vertical lines for each eyebrow. Use the flat side of the burner to add a small shadow near the tip of both sides of the nose. Make four curved lines on each side of the mustache. Add two more lines to define the bottom of the mustache. Make long flowing lines in the beard.

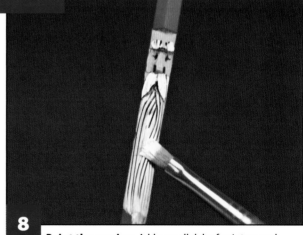

8 **Paint the carving.** Add a small dab of paint on each eyebrow and paint the mustache. Thin the paint for the beard so the burned detail shows through. Carve off a small area of paint on the back of the carving and sign and date your work. You may want to use initials to save space.

Santa pencil pattern

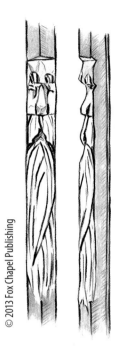

For more information on Ron Johnson, see page 96.

materials & tools

MATERIALS:
- Standard pencil
- Acrylic paint: white or off white

TOOLS:
- Detail knife
- ⅛" (3mm) #11 gouge
- Woodburner
- Old knife
- Small paintbrush

The author used these products for the project. Substitute your choice of brands, tools, and materials as desired.

Experiment with a carpenter's pencil or small dowel to create a variety of quick characters.

5-Minute Owl

Easy beginner project is ideal for teaching and demonstrations

By Jan Oegema

materials & tools

MATERIALS:

• 1" x 1" x 6" basswood or wood of choice
• Finish of choice (I left my owl unfinished, but you could use a clear lacquer or washes of acrylic paint)

TOOLS:

• Carving knife of choice
• Pencil
• Ruler
• ¼" #6 gouge

The author used these products for the project. Substitute your choice of brands, tools, and materials as desired.

This quick little owl is an excellent project that builds confidence and teaches fundamental carving techniques.

The design includes all of the basic cuts: stop cut, push cut, paring cut, chip cut, and stab cut. Unfortunately, I can't take credit for the idea. The design has been around for decades and as the instructions have been passed along from carver to carver, the project has evolved, and the name of the originator has been lost. If you can identify the person responsible, please contact the Fox Chapel Publishing so we can give the proper credit.

I start with a 6"-long blank. This provides plenty of wood to hold as I carve an owl on each end. When the carving is finished, simply cut it from the blank.

1 **Draw in the top of the head.** Measure down ½" on the front and back corners. Sketch a line from the side corners down to these marks. Use the drawings as a guide. This gives you two triangles on opposite sides of the blank.

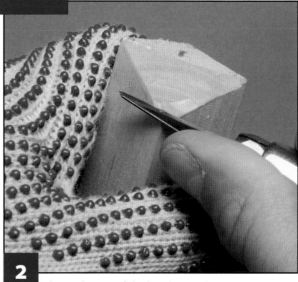

2 **Shape the top of the head.** Use either a push cut or a paring cut to remove the triangles sketched in Step 1. This forms the top of the owl's head. The type of cut you use depends on the grain of the wood and your hand strength.

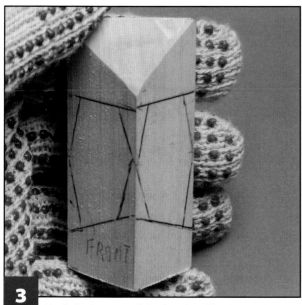

3 **Mark the bottom of the head and body.** Use the drawings as a guide. Draw in the perch and the bottom of the head, and make ⅛"-deep stop cuts along these lines. Mark the sharp corners to remove on the belly, sides, and the back of the head.

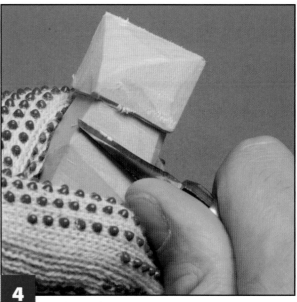

4 **Rough out the owl.** Use a paring cut or a push cut to carve from the middle of the owl's belly, halfway between the perch and the bottom of the head, up to the stop cuts. Use push cuts to remove the sharp corners on the front and sides of the owl, and taper the back of the head.

5 **Sketch in the beak and ears.** Use the drawings as a guide. The ears are defined by long sloping curves across the top and down both sides. The beak is defined by two triangular cuts starting approximately ¼" from the front corner of the blank on either side.

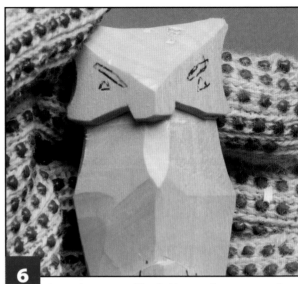

6 **Carve the ears and beak.** Use a push cut to carve along the sloping lines of the ears. Use caution not to chip out the ears. Make stop cuts along the lines of the beak and slice up to the stop cuts to free the chips. Sketch in the eyes, eyebrows, and claws.

7 **Carve the eyes and claws.** Make two small chip cuts on each side of the perch to define the claws. Remove a three-corner chip for each eye. Make two slightly curved angled cuts above the eye for each eyebrow.

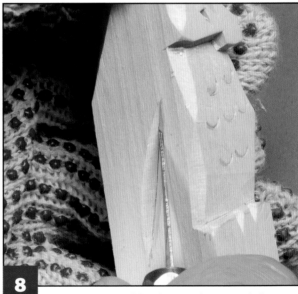

8 **Add the wings and feathers.** Make two angled cuts to define each wing on the back of the blank. Use a ¼" #6 gouge to make stab cuts defining the three rows of feathers on the owl's belly. Apply your finish of choice.

5-minute owl patterns

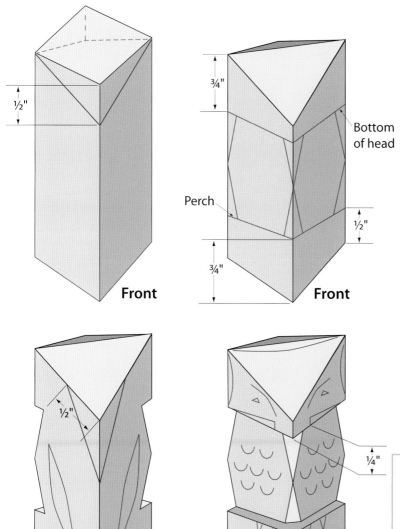

For more information on Jan Oegema, see page 96.

further reading

Teach Yourself Wood Spirit Study Stick Kit
By Jan Oegema

Teach yourself to quickly and easily carve a classic wood spirit with this all-in-one kit that includes a study stick guide, a blank to practice on, and an instructional booklet for carving a wood spirit's eyes, nose, mouth, and ears.

Available for $29.95 from Fox Chapel Publishing, 1970 Broad St., East Petersburg, Pa., 17520, 800-457-9112, www.foxchapelpublishing.com, or check your local retailer.

Hand-Carved Classics

Practice knife carving with a ball-in-cage and chain links

By Kivel Weaver

You don't need a lot of tools to carve a masterpiece; I have carved a variety of things with just a pocketknife—including a variety of chains.

I started whittling and carving at age four when my father gave me my first pocketknife. It was an old rusty relic he had found, but it was a jewel to me. I carved any wood I found lying around.

My first attempt at sharpening was with a rock I picked up off the ground. After sharpening for a while, I was satisfied—and it seemed to cut better. My father borrowed my knife, dulled it, and returned it to me. After I re-sharpened it, my father again asked to borrow it—and I said, "No, you just want to dull it again." He never asked again.

I sold my first carving, a monkey carved from a peach pit, for a quarter when I was ten. Later, I heard about a fellow who whittled working pliers from wood. He wouldn't show me how to make the pliers, but gave me a pair that were broken. I worked for three years before I made my first working pair. Then, I moved on to ball-in-cages and chains.

CARVING A BALL-IN-CAGE

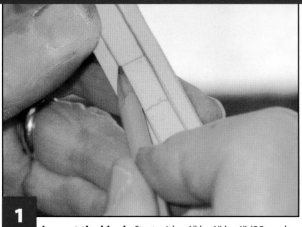

1 **Lay out the blank.** Start with a 1" by 1" by 4" (25mm by 25mm by 102mm) pine block. Mark lines ¼" (6mm) in from each corner. Then, mark lines ½" (13mm) from each end to finish defining the cage. Mark a line 1¼" (32mm) from each end to separate the three balls.

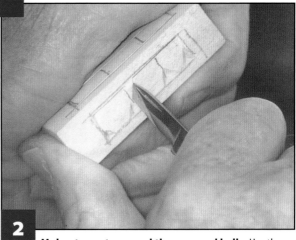

2 **Make stop cuts around the cage and balls.** Use the point of a blade to make ⅛" (3mm)-deep cuts around the edges of the cage and between the balls. Cut out a fairly large triangular chip from each inside corner of the cage. Then, make similar cuts to remove diamond shapes between the balls. Repeat the process on all four sides to rough out the balls.

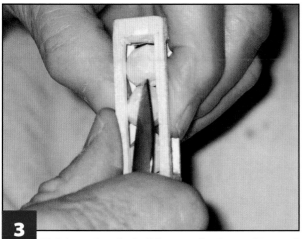

3 **Finish carving the ball-in-cage.** Continue making small cuts to free the balls. Don't carve the balls too small or they will fall out of the cage. After the balls are free, use small shaving cuts to round the balls. Clean up any cuts on the cage walls and smooth the inside top and bottom of the cage. You can also taper the top of the cage for a more finished look.

CARVING A CHAIN

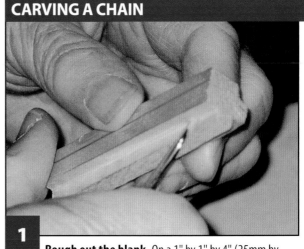

1 **Rough out the blank.** On a 1" by 1" by 4" (25mm by 25mm by 102mm) piece of clear white pine or basswood, mark a line ¼" (6mm) in from each side. Cut along the line with a sharp knife. Remove the ¼" by ¼" (6mm by 6mm) section from each corner, leaving a 4" (100mm)-long cross. Mark the center of the cross on two opposite sides. Then, make two marks 1" (25mm) from each end on the sides not previously marked. This divides the chain into three 2" (51mm)-long links.

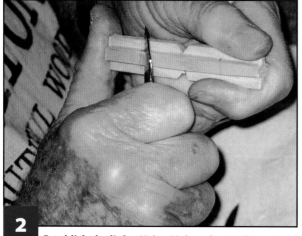

2 **Establish the links.** Make a V-shaped cut at the center mark on both sides. Cut down to the flat of the cross. This establishes two distinct links. Make a V-shaped cut at each of the 1" (25mm) marks. Then, shave the 1" (25mm) end sections down to the flat of the cross on both sides. This establishes the third (middle) link.

3 **Carve the end links.** Use the point of a knife blade to hollow the end links. Then, cut the space between the two links to separate them. Use the tip of a knife to follow the outline where the end links join the center link.

materials & tools

MATERIALS:
- 2 each 1" x 1" x 4" (25mm x 25mm x 102mm) pine or basswood

TOOLS:
- Carving knife

The author used these products for the project. Substitute your choice of brands, tools, and materials as desired.

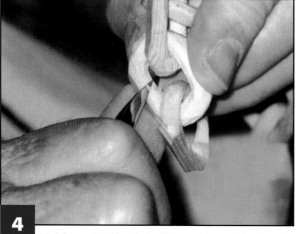

4 **Finish carving the chain.** Keep making small cuts until the links are free. Hollow the center link and continue making small shaving cuts to smooth all three links.

For more information on Kivel Weaver, see page 96.

Combine the Two Projects

Start with a 1" by 1" by 12" (25mm by 25mm by 305mm) blank. Sketch several links, using the method above. Then, lay out a section for a ball-in-cage near the center of the block. Add a few more links, ending with another ball-in-cage. Carve a hook on the end, using the same technique used for the chain, to make it easy to display. Once you get the hang of it, you can combine a number of different elements and complexities in a single chain for a unique work of art. Don't be afraid to experiment and have fun!

5-Minute Wizard

Beginner project is a great introduction to woodcarving

By Tom Hindes

The five-minute wizard is a perfect project for learning basic carving skills and is also well-suited for demonstration purposes. I display carvings at gift shops, festivals, and art fairs; I whittle or carve whenever I get the chance. The five-minute wizard is a simple project that can be given away to spectators. Children especially enjoy receiving a souvenir. I normally carve the wizards while I'm at the event, and then take them home and paint them. I give away the painted ones to onlookers while I carve a supply for the next event.

It may take a bit longer to make your first few wizards, but once you have the steps down, you'll be completing them in about five minutes and can quickly carve a large supply. They make wonderful little gifts for random acts of kindness. Leave one along with your tip at the local restaurant or give one to your favorite cashier. You can also attach a pin back or turn them into key chains.

I create 4" (102mm)-long wizards, but you can adapt the technique to any size carving. Start with a triangular blank (see page 42 for instructions on cutting triangular blanks) and leave a little extra length for easy handling. Once you are comfortable with the technique, experiment with tree branches to make rustic-looking wizards. Make sure your knife is sharp and strop as necessary throughout the carving process.

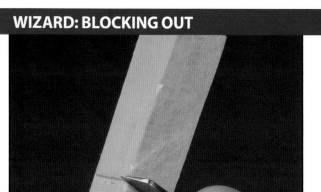

1 **Outline the bottom of the hat.** Make a mark on the corner, 1½" (38mm) down from the top of the blank. Draw angled lines from the mark out to the edges of the blank. Make ⅛" (3mm)-deep stop cuts along these lines with a carving knife.

2 **Relieve the face up to the hat.** Start a slicing cut ¼" (6mm) down from the stop cut on each of the flat surfaces. Cut up to the stop cuts to create the surface for the eye sockets and cheeks.

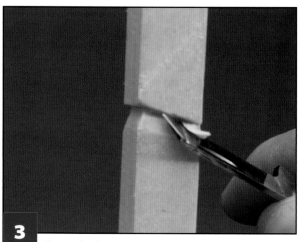

3 **Shape the face.** Position the blade on the outside corner of the blank ¼" (6mm) down from the stop cut. Cut up to the stop cut to remove about ³⁄₁₆" (5mm) from both sides of the face.

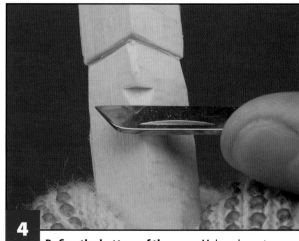

4 **Define the bottom of the nose.** Make a deep stop cut on the front corner, ½" (13mm) to ¾" (19mm) down from the bottom of the hat. Cut up to the stop cut from below to separate the bottom of the nose from the mouth and chin.

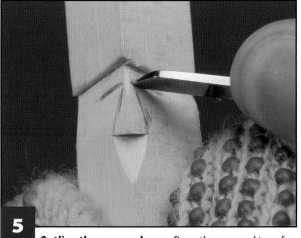

5 **Outline the nose and eyes.** Draw the nose and top of the eyes. Starting at the inside corner of the eye, plunge the knife tip in and cut to the bottom of the nose. Then, start at the inside corner and cut to the outside corner of the eye. Repeat the two stop cuts on the opposite side.

6 **Shape the nose and cheeks.** Using the knife tip, cut up to the stop cuts made in Step 5 and remove a chip from each side of the nose. The deep area where the cuts intersect will be the eye socket. Remove the corners on the bottom of the nose.

WIZARD: ADDING DETAILS

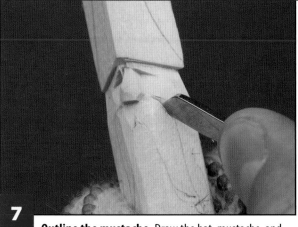

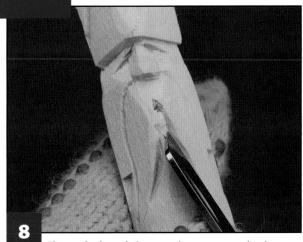

7 **Outline the mustache.** Draw the hat, mustache, and beard. Angle the knife blade toward the mustache and make a stop cut around the mustache. Cut down toward the stop cut to separate the cheeks from the mustache.

8 **Shape the beard.** Cut up to the stop cuts under the mustache. Cut along the beard outline to finish shaping the beard. Go back with the tip of the knife or a small V-tool and add hair lines and texture to the beard and mustache if desired.

9 **Shape the nose.** Give the tip of the nose a rounded or pointed shape. Then, shave down the top to create the bridge of the nose. Cut up from the tip of the nose and free the chip by carving down from the eyebrows. Carve in small semi-circles for the eyes.

10 **Shape the hat.** Use your thumb to push the back of the knife blade and roll the blade back toward you as you cut the hat to a point. You can make the hat long and pointed, squashed down, or even folded at the top. Use your imagination and make it your own.

materials & tools

MATERIALS:
- ¾" x ¾" x 4" (19mm x 19mm x 102mm) basswood ripped in half (Makes two blanks.)
- Acrylic paints of choice (optional)

TOOLS:
- Pencil
- Carving knife (I use a pocketknife)
- Small V-tool (optional)
- Small paintbrushes (optional)

The author used these products for the project. Substitute your choice of brands, tools, and materials as desired.

Finishing Notes

I use acrylic paints to finish the wizards. You can paint them with your own color scheme or leave them natural. Whatever you decide, be sure to erase, carve, or sand away the pencil marks. These marks will often show through layers of paint.

Cutting Triangular Blanks

Set a table saw blade to 45° and cut halfway through a scrap block of wood, such as a 2 by 4. Cut from both directions to create a 45°-angled groove in the middle. Slice halfway down the length of the board through the center of the groove with a band saw.

Clamp the angled jig to the band saw table. Position a square carving blank in the groove and feed the blank through the band saw blade to create two triangular carving blanks.

TIPS **BLADE CONTROL**

For maximum control, position your thumb on the back of the knife blade and use it to push the blade where you want it to go.

For more information on Tom Hindes, see page 96.

Layout Guide for 5-Minute Wizard

From Howard Hawrey, Palm Coast, Fla.

I have carved dozens of Tom Hindes' wizard faces. I learned to cut the blanks and carve the wizard quickly, but laying out the guidelines still took some time.

I devised this simple jig to expedite the layout process. The jig fits nicely in your toolbox and is made from a piece of ¾"-wide by 4"-long (19mm by 102mm) aluminum angle iron. Aluminum angle iron is available in 3' (915mm)-long sections for less than $5 at most home improvement stores.

Cut the angle iron to length with a 20° angle on one side. The angled end at the top of the jig should look like the peak of a roof. Measure down ½" (13mm) and 1½" (38mm) from the peak at the top of the jig. Make marks at both of these measurements. Cut across the corner at each mark with a hacksaw. The cuts should be about ¼" (6mm) deep.

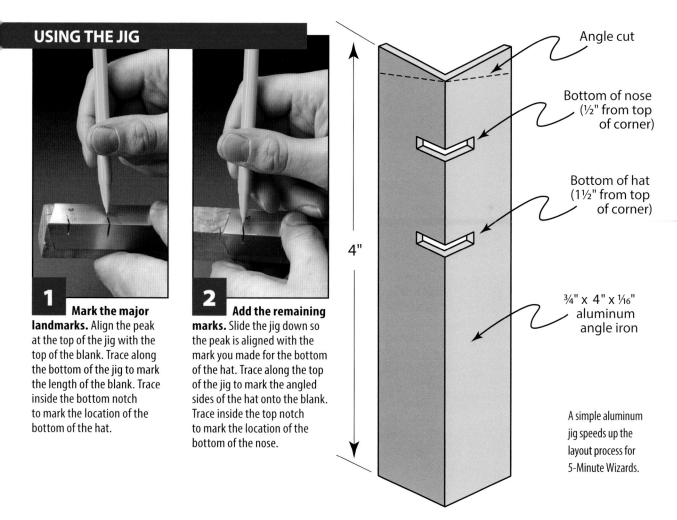

USING THE JIG

1 Mark the major landmarks. Align the peak at the top of the jig with the top of the blank. Trace along the bottom of the jig to mark the length of the blank. Trace inside the bottom notch to mark the location of the bottom of the hat.

2 Add the remaining marks. Slide the jig down so the peak is aligned with the mark you made for the bottom of the hat. Trace along the top of the jig to mark the angled sides of the hat onto the blank. Trace inside the top notch to mark the location of the bottom of the nose.

Angle cut

Bottom of nose (½" from top of corner)

Bottom of hat (1½" from top of corner)

4"

¾" x 4" x ¹⁄₁₆" aluminum angle iron

A simple aluminum jig speeds up the layout process for 5-Minute Wizards.

Twisted Spiral
Ornament

Carve this seemingly complex design in eight easy steps

By Carol Kent

This project provides good practice for working with the grain and developing knife-carving skills. Once you master the basics, you'll find yourself incorporating the design into other carvings.

It is much easier to cut off a corner than it is to cut across a flat plane. In this project, we will be constantly creating corners, which will later be removed.

I developed my method for carving these spirals in my first year of carving. My instructor had us carve a spiral that had two strands and wrapped around twice as many times. To carve that, you cut the pattern lines deeper and deeper with the knife tip. This was dangerous and difficult, so I adapted his design.

Since then, I have carved spirals using between two and six strands in everything from a walking stick to a toothpick. My favorite use of the design is the 2½"- to 3"-long three-strand version, which I make into earrings.

Start with a 1" by 1" by 6" (25mm by 25mm by 152mm) blank. Be as precise as possible when cutting. Precise blanks will produce an easier, more attractive finished product. After cutting it to size, run a straight line from all four corners to the center of one end. Cut along these lines to shape the blank into a pyramid.

ORNAMENT: LAYING OUT THE SPIRAL

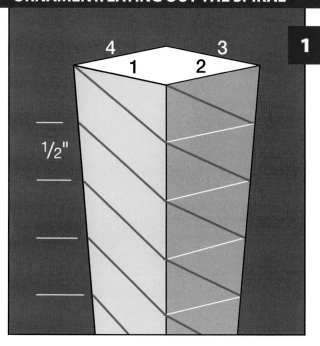

1 **Lay out the spiral.** Mark the sides (1 to 4) on the top of the blank. Use an ink gel pen (which doesn't smudge like a pencil). Mark down the length of the ornament on each side at ½" (13mm) increments to about 1½" (38mm) from the pyramid tip. Hold a straight edge at the top corner of side 1 to the first mark on side 2. Use the same procedure to mark a line from the top corner of side 2 to the first mark on side 3, and continue around the blank. Following this procedure, the line will go from a high point on the left to a lower point on the right. Check the pattern by looking at each side—there should be a continuous line running from each corner down the length of the ornament.

ORNAMENT: CARVING THE SPIRAL

2 **Cut off the first corners.** Start at the first mark on any side and cut a diagonal wedge at the corner, removing the pattern line. Repeat the same procedure down the length of the ornament. You will be cutting bigger wedges at the top of the ornament and smaller wedges as you approach the tip of the ornament. Follow the same procedure on all four sides.

3 **Connect the corner wedges.** Cut more wedges across the flat sides to connect the corners. This should remove all of the pattern lines. Deepen all of the cuts, especially on the thicker end.

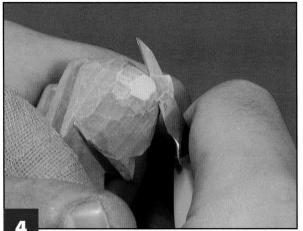

4 **Round the top of the spiral.** Take a healthy chip off each corner of the blank. This will create four new corners that will each be removed. Continue removing corners until the top is rounded to your satisfaction.

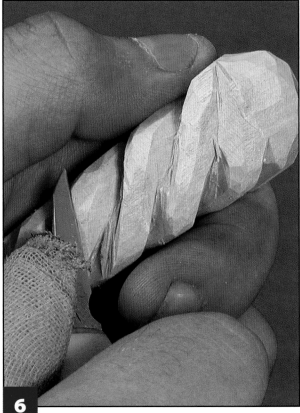

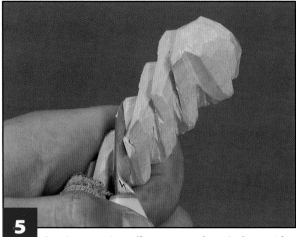

5 **Continue cutting off corners on the spiral part.** After all the corners are cut off, the piece is roughed out. Deepen all the channels, one after another, more aggressively at the top. Continue rounding the strands as you deepen the channels.

6 **Smooth the corners.** As you cut the channels deeper, you will be creating an edge along the surface of the blank. Trim these corners off to get smoother, more delicate strands. Do not sharpen the tip of the spiral until the carving is almost finished. Be careful—you should be close to cutting through the center. The goal is to cut through to the center of the top and bottom of the ornament at the same time. If you want to sand your ornament smooth, now is the time.

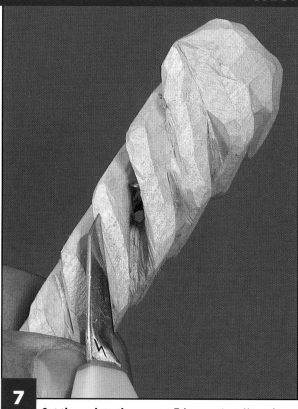

7 **Cut through to the center.** Take your time. Up to this point, we've been whittling pretty aggressively. As soon as the center is breached, the ornament loses a lot of its structural integrity and becomes very fragile. Make lighter cuts and be gentle when you are holding the ornament. You may want to set it aside and pick it up again when your hands are fresh.

8 **Thin the strands from the inside.** Use a detail knife, if desired. A larger opening in the center produces a more delicate end product. Insert a small eye screw in the center of the top. To bring out the grain, dip the ornament in golden oak stain and gently wipe it. Allow the stain to dry thoroughly, and then double-dip the spiral in Deft or a clear finish. Wipe off any finish that drips off the tip.

materials & tools

MATERIALS:
- 1" x 1" x 6" (25mm x 25mm x 152mm) basswood blank
- Deft clear finish
- Stain (optional)
- Sandpaper, 220 grit (optional)
- Small eye screw

TOOLS:
- Ruler
- Gel pen
- Carving knife
- Detail knife (optional)

The author used these products for the project. Substitute your choice of brands, tools, and materials as desired.

For more information on Carol Kent, see page 96.

Back Scratcher

Indulge yourself with these decorative yet functional pieces

by Chris Lubkemann

I don't know about you, but in my opinion a backscratcher is an intensely useful and practical item. Granted, it may be a little tough to carry around throughout an average working day, but at least you can keep it next to your favorite recliner while you're watching the evening news or a good basketball game. With pinpoint precision, you can get at that itch in the middle of your back just below your shoulder blades without getting up to go scratch it on the corner of a kitchen cabinet. And you definitely don't want to ask your wife to scratch your back if she's an alumna of the team that's down by six points with 1.5 seconds left on the clock! Who knows what permanent damage she might do!

1 Naturally, there are different shapes and different degrees of sharpness, depending on the type of scratching you want to do. For superprecise, light, pinpoint scratching, you can carve a sharp-beaked, Dr. Seuss-type head, such as the red-crested critter in the middle. For harder, firmer, all-over scratching, I'd suggest a round-billed duck head. We'll use as our starting blank the piece on the left and aim for a broad-spectrum scratcher, sharp enough to be precise, but not so sharp as to tear clothing or skin when medium to firm pressure is applied.

2 Taper both sides of the topknot branch, cutting the same amount from both sides.

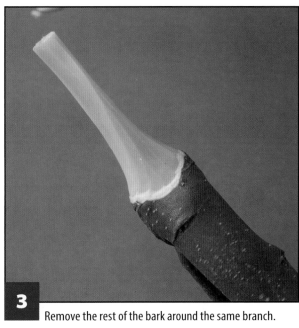

3 Remove the rest of the bark around the same branch.

4 Remove the bark around the beak branch and taper the branch a little from both sides.

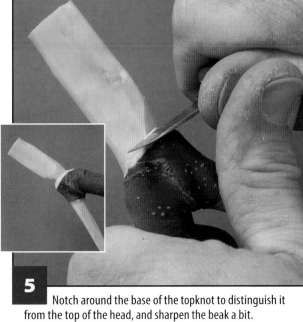

5 Notch around the base of the topknot to distinguish it from the top of the head, and sharpen the beak a bit.

6 Curve the top of the topknot slightly and sharpen it a bit from the sides.

7 Make some V-notches in the topknot, or crest, or whatever you want to call it.

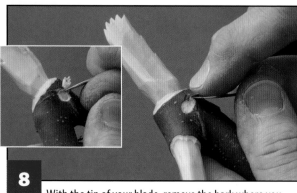

8 With the tip of your blade, remove the bark where you want the eyes.

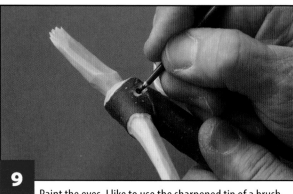

9 Paint the eyes. I like to use the sharpened tip of a brush handle.

10 Here's the working end of your backscratcher. Of course, you can add all kinds of detail and personality with some creative painting!

materials & tools

MATERIALS:
- Forked branch of choice
- Acrylic paints of choice (optional)

TOOLS:
- Knife
- Sandpaper—a couple of grits on the fine to very fine side (150- and 220-grit would work).
- Pencil, pen, or marker

The author used these products for the project.
Substitute your choice of brands, tools, and materials as desired.

For more information on Chris Lubkemann, see page 96.

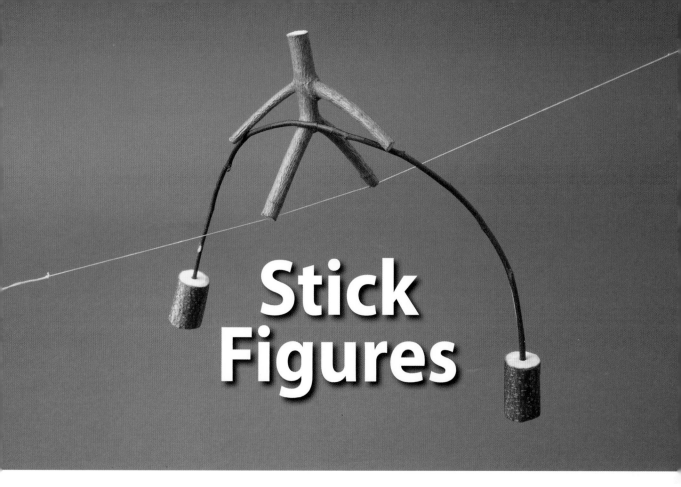

Stick Figures

Carve creative little people with personalities

by Chris Lubkemann

Over the past four or five decades, as I've hiked through woods or rummaged through branch piles of one description and origin or another, I've stumbled on an amazing variety of almost-already-carved stick figures. Every natural stick figure (at least the "human" type) has a head, a trunk, two arms, and two legs. The position these have grown in determines what the character is doing. Over the years I've come across some good ones: a discus thrower, a shortstop fielding a hot grounder, a runner carrying the Olympic torch, a gymnast performing a floor exercise move, a soccer player making a perfect trap of the ball, and more.

To some of the basic formations, I've done practically nothing. They've remained in the condition in which I found them. Others I've tweaked a little with my pocketknife and some kind of pen or marker. In the following series of photos, we'll create a tightrope walker.

Once you develop an instinct for stick figures, you almost don't have to look for them. They just about jump out at you! You might even want to develop a stick figure collection. See how many different characters you can find.

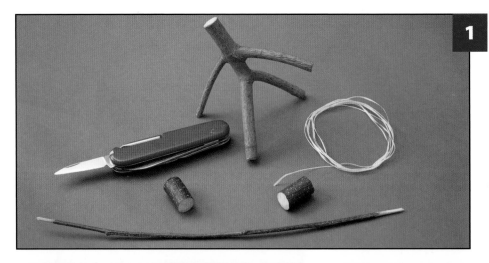

1 With this little maple branch, some dental floss (that's all we could lay our hands on at the photo studio!), and a few more little pieces, let's go for a tightrope walker.

2 Make holes in one end of each of the two little fat "logs."

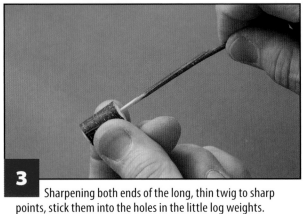

3 Sharpening both ends of the long, thin twig to sharp points, stick them into the holes in the little log weights.

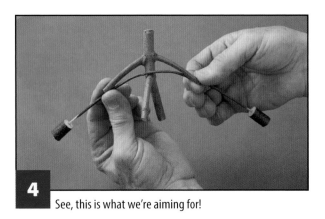

4 See, this is what we're aiming for!

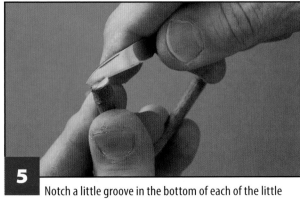

5 Notch a little groove in the bottom of each of the little man's feet. There's no safety net, and you definitely don't want him to slip off the "tightfloss"!

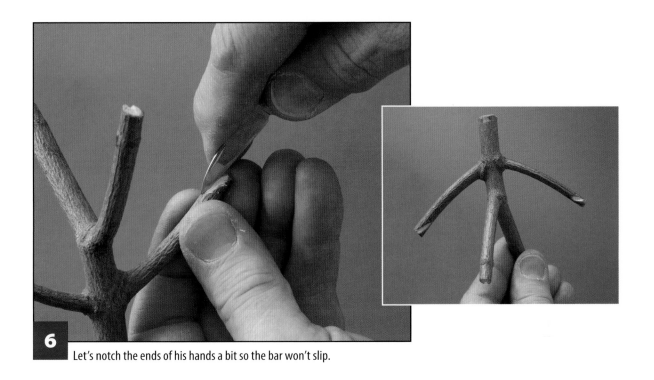

6 Let's notch the ends of his hands a bit so the bar won't slip.

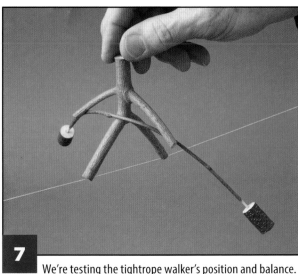

7 We're testing the tightrope walker's position and balance. Oops! We didn't make his balancing rod long enough to create the correct center of gravity.

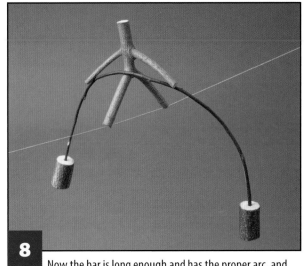

8 Now the bar is long enough and has the proper arc, and our little performer is ready to do his act!

Classic
Ball-in-Cage

This old-time whittling project is fun to carve and a real attention-getter

By Addison "Dusty" Dussinger

This impressive-looking project is actually quite simple to create. Once you master the basic techniques, you'll find dozens of ways to use the intriguing project. Add one to a walking stick or a lovespoon, or incorporate several together in a chain.

I developed an easy way to draw the cage on the block using a few measurements and a ribbon as a template. With a little bit of practice, you'll be able to sketch one on and be carving in no time.

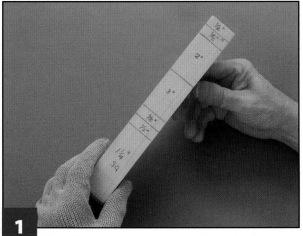

1 **Mark the measurements on the blank.** Use the guidelines on page 57. A ruler and square will give you the most accurate lines. Label the center of each side from A to D on the top and bottom of the blank. Leave the blank long so you have something to hold onto.

2 **Carve off the corners of the block.** You want to make the block octagonal (eight-sided), but keep the sides as flat as possible right now. If you happen to carve off your label, be sure to re-mark it as soon as you finish carving off the corners. Always wear a thumb guard and carving glove for safety. Transfer the lines onto the freshly carved sides.

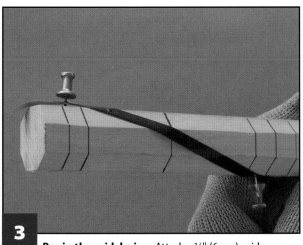

3 **Begin the grid design.** Attach a ¼" (6mm)-wide ribbon to the top section of side A with a thumbtack. Wrap the ribbon down around the blank, and attach it to bottom section of side C with another thumbtack. Trace along both sides of the ribbon. Leaving the tack in place on A, rewrap the ribbon in the opposite direction and tack again at the bottom of C. Trace both sides of the ribbon.

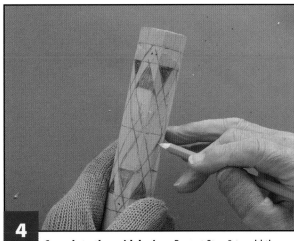

4 **Complete the grid design.** Repeat Step 3 to add the grids from the tops of sides B, C, and D. When you are done, the blank will show a series of diamonds and triangles. Shade in the end sections that will be carved clear through the blank. Leave about 2" (51mm) in the center unshaded to allow wood for the ball.

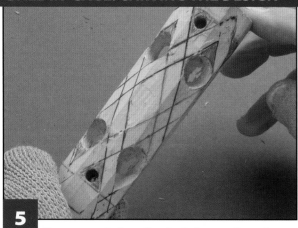

5 **Remove waste from the shaded areas.** Use various sizes of drill bits to clear out some of the waste. Make stop cuts around the cage bars. Work your way out from the drilled holes and clear out the diamonds and triangles. Be careful not to split the bars; the grain changes often in a project like this, and the bars are fragile.

6 **Begin to remove the waste around the ball.** Carefully relieve the wood down to the proposed thickness of the ball. Do not remove a lot of wood—you want the ball to be as large as possible while still clearing the cage. As you get close to the cage, take care that you don't split the thin wood.

7 **Continue removing the waste around the ball.** Take your time, and round the edges of the ball as much as possible. Carefully undercut the bars to free the ball; it is a difficult area to carve. When you've carved away enough wood, the ball will slide free inside the cage.

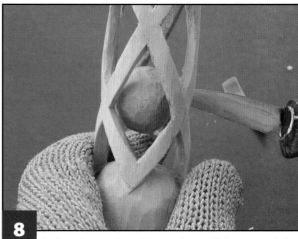

8 **Refine the carving.** Take small cuts off the cage and the ball to smooth out any rough places. You want the ball to be able to travel from one end of the cage to the other without stopping.

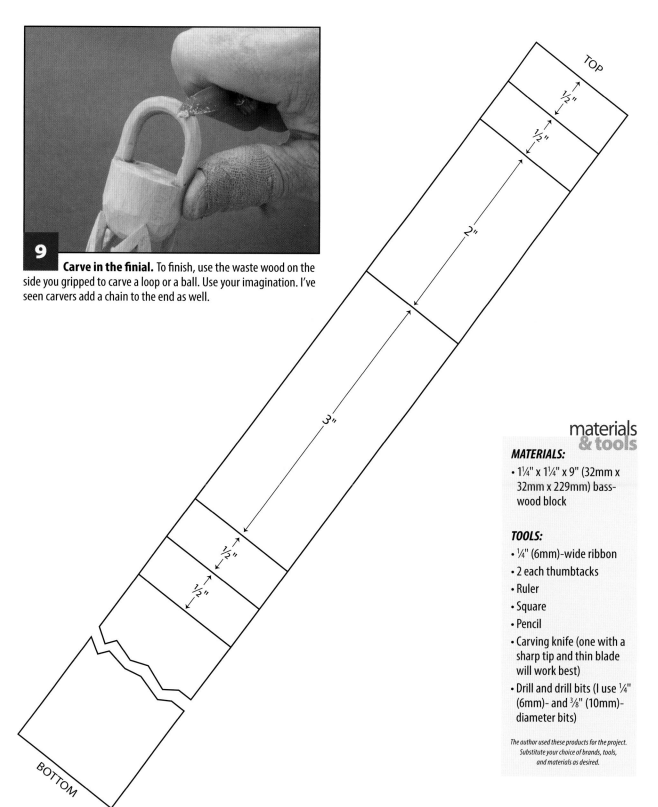

9 **Carve in the finial.** To finish, use the waste wood on the side you gripped to carve a loop or a ball. Use your imagination. I've seen carvers add a chain to the end as well.

TOP

½"

½"

2"

3"

½"

½"

BOTTOM

materials
& tools

MATERIALS:

• 1¼" x 1¼" x 9" (32mm x 32mm x 229mm) basswood block

TOOLS:

• ¼" (6mm)-wide ribbon
• 2 each thumbtacks
• Ruler
• Square
• Pencil
• Carving knife (one with a sharp tip and thin blade will work best)
• Drill and drill bits (I use ¼" (6mm)- and ⅜" (10mm)-diameter bits)

The author used these products for the project. Substitute your choice of brands, tools, and materials as desired.

Ball-in-cage guidelines

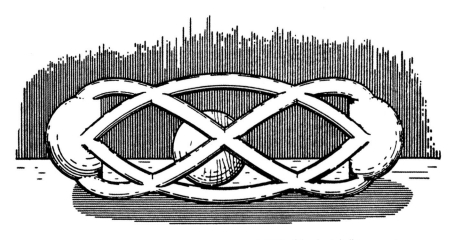

A sketch of the classic ball-in-cage on which this project was based.

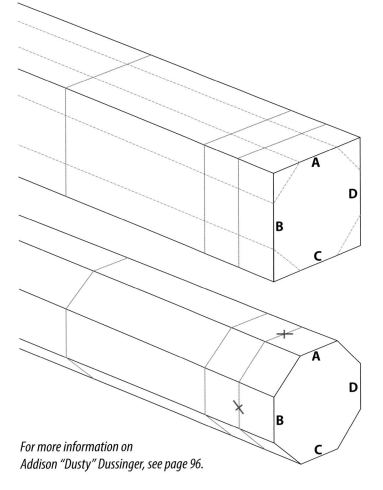

Remove the corners (marked in blue) to form an octagon. (See Step 2.)

Begin on side A and tack the ribbon on the first line down from the top of the blank (marked with a red X). Wrap the ribbon around to the opposite side (C) from both directions. Repeat the process on all four sides. (See Step 3.)

For more information on Addison "Dusty" Dussinger, see page 96.

Make a Musical Frog

This fast and fun project is a unique musical instrument

By Everett Ellenwood

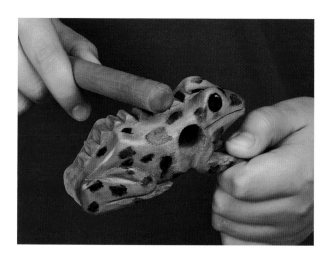

This carving is meant to be handled. People won't be able to resist picking it up to see what sound it makes. When you rub the stick along the frog's back, it makes a delightful croaking sound. The sound varies depending on which direction you rub the stick.

The musical frog is a great project to introduce kids to woodcarving. The simple design can be carved quickly, and kids love the sound it makes.

To get started, transfer the pattern to the block of wood and cut the blank on a band saw or with a coping saw.

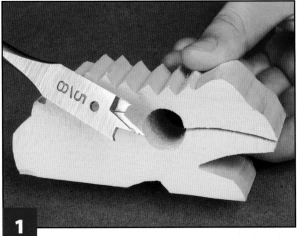

1 **Prepare the blank.** Mark the location of the hole and draw the mouth. Drill the hole with a ⅝" (16mm)-diameter spade bit. Cut along the mouth line back to the hole with a band saw or coping saw. Measure and make several marks halfway across the thickness of the blank. Connect the marks to draw a centerline the entire way around the frog.

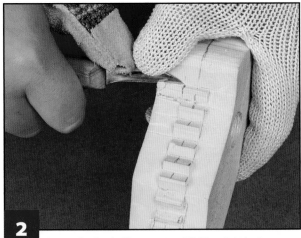

2 **Carve the back.** Measure over ¼" (6mm) on both sides of the centerline in the ribbed area. Use a backsaw to cut down to the depth of the ribs on both sides of the centerline. Remove the wood from both sides with a carving knife, leaving the ribs ½" (13mm) wide.

MUSICAL FROG: SHAPING THE PROJECT

3 **Carve the head.** Draw the shape of the head onto the blank. Use the centerline to make sure it is balanced on both sides. Round the head and top of the face with a knife.

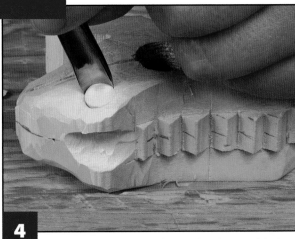

4 **Carve the eyes.** Remove the wood on the top of the head between the protruding eyes with a ⅜" (10mm) #9 gouge. Plunge the same gouge into the wood and work it around in a circle to form the eyes.

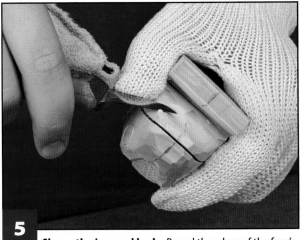

5 **Shape the jaw and body.** Round the edges of the frog's jaw with a carving knife. Then, round the edges of the body.

6 **Define the back legs.** Trace the outline of the back legs with a V-tool. Use a gouge to lower the body around the legs.

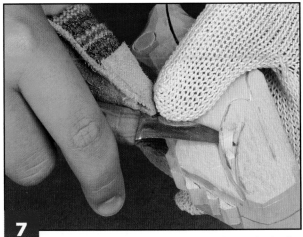

7 **Round the legs.** Round and shape the legs with a knife. Compare the two legs to each other to keep the frog symmetrical.

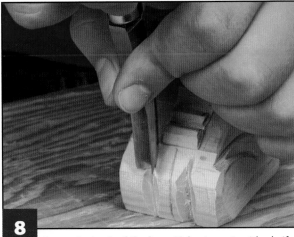

8 **Carve the back of the legs.** Make stop cuts with a knife or backsaw and use a V-tool to shape the back of the legs.

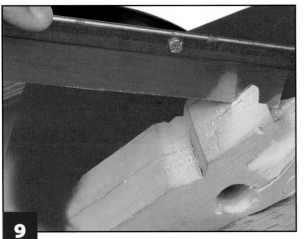

9 **Carve the front legs.** Use a backsaw to separate the front legs, and then round and shape the legs with a knife.

materials
& tools

MATERIALS:

- 1½" x 2" x 4½" (38mm x 51mm x 114mm) basswood
- ⅝"-diameter x 5"-long (16mm x 127mm) dowel
- 220- and 320-grit sandpaper
- Acrylic paints: green, black, and white
- Gloss spray varnish

TOOLS:

- Band saw or coping saw
- ⅜" (10mm) #9 gouge
- V-tool
- Backsaw
- Carving knife
- Ruler
- Drill with ⅝" (16mm)-diameter spade bit

The author used these products for the project. Substitute your choice of brands, tools, and materials as desired.

For more information on Everett Ellenwood, see page 96.

MUSICAL FROG: FINISHING THE PROJECT

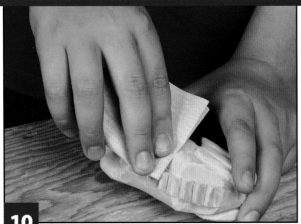

10 **Sand the frog.** Sand the surface of the frog with 220- and then 320-grit sandpaper. Remove the sanding dust.

11 **Paint the frog and dowel.** Use acrylic paint. After the paint dries, spray the surface with gloss varnish for a wet look.

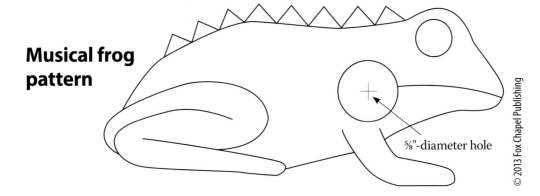

Musical frog pattern

⅝"-diameter hole

© 2013 Fox Chapel Publishing

Simple Starter Santa

Spread holiday cheer with this basic design

By Kathleen Schuck

This simple Santa can be carved in a day. It is a great project to become familiar with the position of facial features and is ideal for beginning carvers.

The project was inspired by a 74-year-old woman in one of my classes. She wanted to jump right into carving Santas. I was not sure she had the hand strength to complete the normal class Santa in the time allotted. Not wanting to disappoint my new student, I set out to design a simple Santa. My student was successful, and I have since carved several to test different color schemes for more elaborate Santas.

Most of my Santas are carved from a 2" by 3" by 6" piece of basswood—it's a comfortable size to handle. Start by making a photocopy of the pattern. Trace the outside design onto the blank with graphite paper. Cut out the perimeter with a band saw, and replace the pattern over the blank to trace in the details.

Consider a pencil your #1 tool and mark the depth you want various parts of the Santa to be. Use an X to mark areas where you want to remove wood.

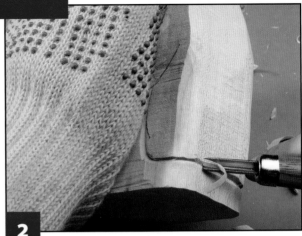

1 **Remove the band saw marks.** Use a carving knife to remove the sharp corners from the sides and back of the Santa. Round the sides. Use a ½" (13mm) #3 gouge for areas that are wider than your knife. Carve the back and front so the hood of the cloak comes to a peak in the middle of the 2" (51mm) thickness.

2 **Rough out the cloak.** Make stop cuts along the pattern lines of the cloak, arms, and hands with a ¼" (6mm) V-tool. Use a knife to further define the stop cuts above and below the arms. Shave up to the stop cut at the bottom of the cloak and below the hands with a ½" (13mm) #3 gouge so it looks like the cloak is over Santa's robe.

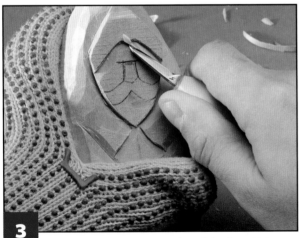

3 **Remove wood from both sides of the face.** Make a stop cut around the beard with a knife. Cut the wood away from the stop cuts on both sides of the face. Round the arms into the stop cuts above and below the arms. Remove wood from around the cowl to separate it from the cloak. Make a stop cut around the cowl just above the forehead and remove enough wood so it looks as if the head goes into and under the cowl.

4 **Make stop cuts around the facial details (see Tip on page 67).** Make a deep stop cut at the eye line above the nose. Make stop cuts along the cheek lines bordering the nose and top of the mustache. Taper the edges of the cheeks up to the stop cut. Angle the knife and cut the chip free at the top of the nose. Make a stop cut along the bottom of the mustache and taper the beard up to mustache.

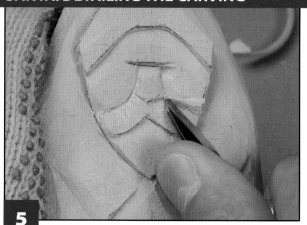

5 **Remove the sharp corners.** Make a stop cut around the tip of the nose. Round and shape the entire mustache to give it a smooth flowing shape. Round and taper the forehead and cowl down into the cape. The cowl should be separated from, but flow toward, the cloak. Separate the hands by removing a wedge of wood from between them.

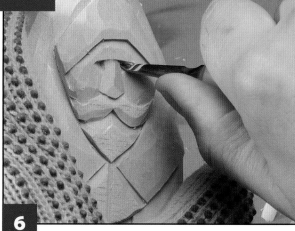

6 **Shape the eyes.** Hold the knife at an angle and slide the tip into the eye socket alongside the nose with the blade pointing toward the outside of the face. Flick your wrist to bring the blade upward to cut a triangular chip from the nose to the stop cut at the eye line. Use the same technique to carve the other eye.

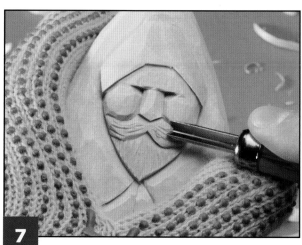

7 **Round the cheeks and the nose.** Round the nose down into the eye sockets with a knife. Round and shape the tip of the nose. Use the knife to round the cheeks down to the stop cuts on the outside of the face where the face meets the cloak. Use a V-tool to add hair lines for the beard and mustache.

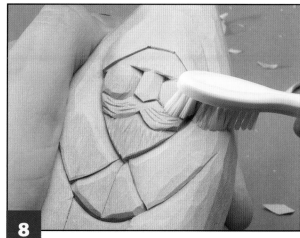

8 **Clean the carving.** Brush the carving with an old clean toothbrush. If there are fingerprints, pencil marks, or dirt marks from oily hands, spray the carving with mild cleanser and brush the soiled areas with the toothbrush. Rinse the carving in lukewarm water. Pat the carving and start painting before the carving dries. This prevents the grain from raising too much.

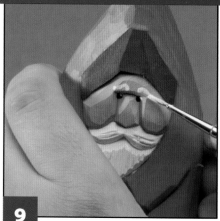

9 **Paint the Santa.** Add a few drops of peach-colored paint to the palette well and fill the well with water. Stir it, and then paint the hands and face. Use white for the beard and inner robe, thinned light red for the cape, and thinned dark red for the cowl. Put a dot of black paint in each chip-carved eye and add a tiny white dot at 11 o'clock or 7 o'clock.
Add the white eyebrows.

materials & tools

MATERIALS:
- 2" x 3" x 6" (51mm x 76mm x 152mm) basswood
- Graphite paper
- Pencil with a new eraser (eraser print)
- Mild cleanser (optional)
- Acrylic paints: light red, dark red, white, peach, and black

TOOLS:
- Band saw
- Carving knife
- ½" (13mm) #3 gouge
- ¼" (6mm) V-tool
- Toothbrush
- Paintbrushes
- Paint palette

The author used these products for the project.
Substitute your choice of brands, tools, and materials as desired.

10 **Stamp the inner robe.** Cut a design into a soft new pencil eraser. Spread a bit of paint on the flat center of the palette, dip the eraser into the paint, and press the eraser onto the inner robe. I usually get two or three prints from each dip.

For more information on Kathleen Schuck, see page 96.

Simple Santa pattern

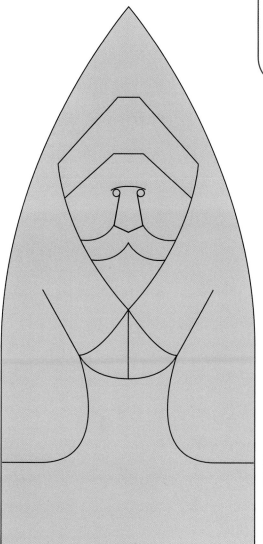

© 2013 Fox Chapel Publishing

Under and Over
Achieving depth and dimension is important in any carving. Think of what goes over (or outside) and under (or inside) on the carving. The mustache is under the nose and over the beard, so remove wood accordingly. Santa's hands are over his cloak and go into his sleeves. Even subtle layers or depths add to the proportions of a carving.

Whittling a Walking Stick

by Chris Lubkemann

A number of years ago when the new Sarasota Middle School in Florida was being built, a whole citrus grove was cleared to make room for it. Needless to say, the bulldozers made mountains and mountains of wonderful raw material. (Citrus wood is great for this type of carving. Florida residents, keep your eyes peeled for rising middle schools or whatever!) Out of the piles of fallen trees and branches came a number of things, not the least useful of which was the crutch I made to help me hobble around after a basketball injury. I think it might have been from the same pile of wood that I got the very nice cane that is currently hanging in my shop.

I'm sure there are many volumes that have been written on walking sticks. I definitely don't consider myself even the slightest expert on carving them, and I'm certainly not trying in any way to compete with all the great walking stick literature that's already out there. All I want to do is suggest a simple project that some folks might enjoy as they hike along some portion of their "journey."

Not too long ago, one of my neighbors topped several of his maple trees. I think all of these particular walking stick blanks came from the huge pile of branches in his backyard. While none of them is perfectly straight (they really don't need to be), they're all thick enough to support a decent amount of weight. Remember, as you choose a branch for your walking stick, pick a species of wood that is hard enough and thick enough to be reliable.

materials & tools

MATERIALS:
- Straight-grained wood of choice

TOOLS:
- Knife
- Sandpaper—a couple of grits on the fine to very fine side (150- and 220-grit would work).

The author used these products for the project. Substitute your choice of brands, tools, and materials as desired.

1 Here are the heads of two walking stick blanks. We'll work on the straight one in my hand.

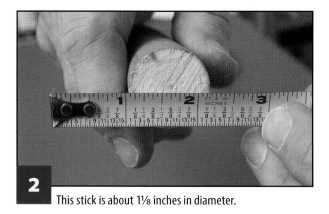

2 This stick is about 1⅛ inches in diameter.

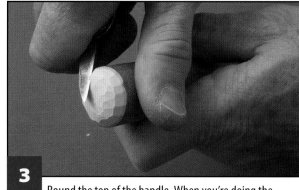

3 Round the top of the handle. When you're doing the drawing cuts for this part, make sure you keep your thumb lower on the branch so that, when your blade does its follow-through jump after clearing the wood, it doesn't do a little operation on your thumb! Some folks like to use thumb guards or tape. I personally don't. However, I've learned to position my thumb so it's out of the way of speeding and jumping knife blades.

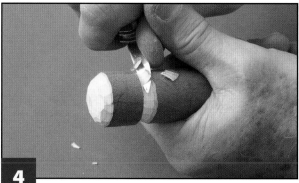

4 By making a wider V-groove ring than you carved in the knife or fork handles, create a knob.

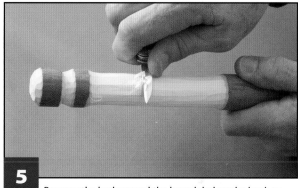

5 Remove the bark around the branch below the knob to form your handgrip.

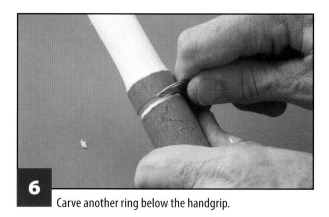

6 Carve another ring below the handgrip.

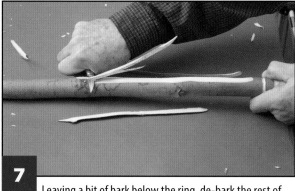

7 Leaving a bit of bark below the ring, de-bark the rest of the walking stick. (If you do this while the wood is still fresh, it's a lot easier.)

Whittling a Decorative
Fishing Lure

Simple project makes a fun display or gift item

By Lora S. Irish

Whittling is individually expressive and uniquely creative—it is a perfect way for beginners to learn the love of working wood, for intermediate carvers to hone their skills, and for advanced carvers to enjoy the challenge of returning to one-knife work.

This whimsical whittled wonder is a decorative folk-art style fishing lure. Fish decoys and lures were once necessary tools for providing food for the table. You could add real hooks and turn the project into a functioning lure, but I created it as a decorative item.

Using simple shapes, a few carved accents and details, a bit of added wood or copper for fins, and one knife, you can carve a vintage-style fishing lure.

If you are a new woodcarver, try using basswood for this project. Although classified as a hardwood, basswood is soft and easy to cut, with a tight fine grain. Its clean white coloring accepts paints well.

Start by removing the sharp corners of the square blank. Draw a centerline and round the blank toward the centerline to give the blank a rough pillow shape.

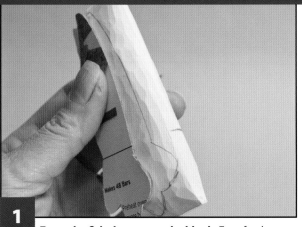

1   **Trace the fish shape onto the blank.** Transfer the outline of the fish's body onto a piece of thin cardboard to create a template. Cut the template and trace the shape of the fish onto one side of the blank. Transfer the location of the front of the two fins and the center of the tail onto the opposite side. Use these marks to position the template correctly and trace the template onto the other side.

2   **Rough out the carving.** Carve away the excess wood around the back, belly, snout, and tail. Taper the sides of the face slightly. Roll the knife quickly along the curved tail to get a smooth cut. Create sharp corners by cutting into the area from two directions.

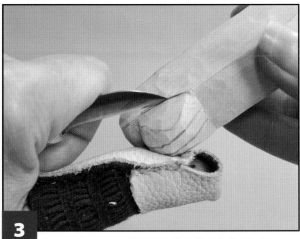

3   **Carve the top and bottom fins.** Sketch the thickness of the fins and the line where the fins join the body. Stop-cut along the line where the fins join the body. Then, carve the wood down to the marked thickness.

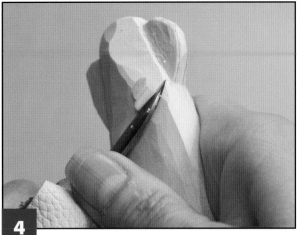

4   **Shape the sides.** Minnows, which most fishing lures represent, are relatively thin. The head and tail are thinner than the chest and belly. Sketch the shape of the head and tail, which are both V-shaped, and carve off the excess wood. Taper the wood toward the head and tail.

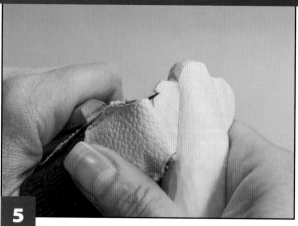

5 **Finish carving the fins.** Taper the top and bottom fins toward the outer edge. The thickest part of the fin is close to the body. Carve a series of V-shaped notches in the fins.

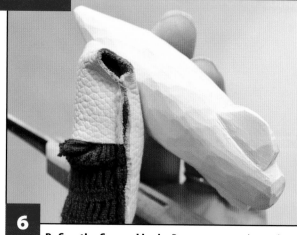

6 **Refine the fins and body.** Remove any rough wood where the fins meet the body by making small cuts with a sharp knife held at a shallow angle. Then, press the back side of the knife blade (the blunt side) across the joint line to press in any stray fibers. Round the sharp edges of the fins where the fins meet the body.

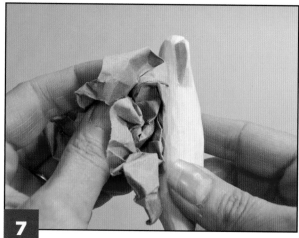

7 **Remove any remaining rough areas.** Use a sharp knife to remove any remaining rough areas. Then, buff the carving with a crumpled brown paper bag. The bag is abrasive enough to remove dirt and other marks from the carving without removing any of the knife-cut planes.

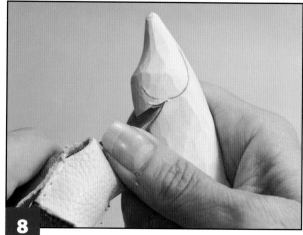

8 **Add the gills.** Use the pattern as a guide to position a penny on the side of the fish; trace around the penny to outline a gill. Extend the gill to the underside of the mouth. Make a stop cut along the gill line. Cut up to the stop cut from the body to separate the gill from the body. Smooth the body down into the gill slit. Repeat on the other side of the fish.

9 **Carve the wooden tail add-on.** Trace the tail pattern onto the tail blank. Alternatively, use a penny to draw two half-circles side by side, and then extend the lines from the half circles to create a rough heart shape. Carve the outline of the tail with a knife, but do not carve the notch where the tail meets the body.

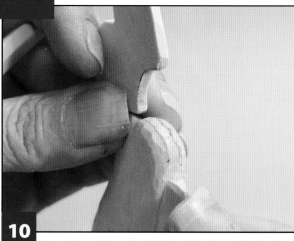

10 Shape the notch on the tail. Trace the shape of the back end of the fish across the point of the heart on the tail blank. Carve away all but ⅛" (3mm) of the wood outside the pencil mark. Use 220-grit sandpaper to smooth the inside of the cut area and to lightly round the sharp edges. Mark the thickness of the tail onto the lure body.

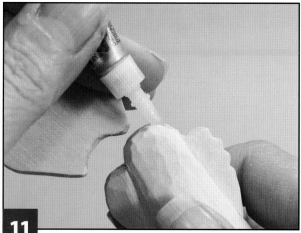

11 **Attach the tail fin.** Use the tip of a knife to carve away a bit of the wood inside the lines marked for the tail. Make several small cuts, creating a shallow groove. Fit the tail into the groove and use 220-grit sandpaper to smooth the groove. Remove any sander dust with an old toothbrush, and test the fit again. When the tail fits properly, attach it to the lure with cyanoacrylate (CA) glue or wood glue. Refine the area where the tail meets the body.

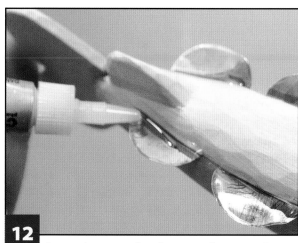

12 **Create the copper fins.** Trace around a penny twice on a sheet of thin copper. Cut the circles with craft scissors and cut each circle in half. Flatten the copper with flat-nose pliers. Carve a thin groove two-thirds to three-quarters of the way down each side of the body, starting behind the gill and ending about ¼" (6mm) from the tail. Slide the copper fins into the grooves and lock them in place with CA glue.

Painting the Lure

Basecoat the lure with two coats of thinned black acrylic paint. Mix a half-brushful of burnt sienna paint with a quarter-size puddle of titanium white, and apply two coats of the reddish-white mixture to the belly, bottom fin, underside of the face, and gill areas. Some black will be visible through this paint. Add a little medium green to the white mixture and apply two light coats to the rest of the lure.

Mix equal parts burnt sienna and medium green to make a dark green-brown mixture. Apply two coats of this mixture to the top third of the lure's body and to the top fin and tail. Allow the paint to dry for a half-hour. Put some pale yellow paint onto your palette and pull the paint into a flat thin layer with a brush. Dip a pencil with a new eraser into the thin layer of yellow paint. Use the eraser like a stamp to make a line of dots down the back of the fish's body on both sides. You can make two spots with each eraser dip in the paint. Clean the yellow off the eraser and use the same technique to add two white eyes on the face. Cut the graphite off the other end of the pencil and sand the end with 220-grit sandpaper to form a scant ⅛" (3mm) circle. Use the tip of the pencil and the dot technique to add small red spots under the lines of yellow dots and black pupils in the center of the white eyes. Allow the paint to dry overnight.

To distress the carving, rub 220-grit sandpaper over the entire fish to remove some of the top layers of paint and, in places, all of the paint to expose bare wood. To catch the prey fish's attention, you can add metallic gold or silver fish scales to the belly area of the lure using a permanent marking pen. Finish the lure with a coat of gloss spray acrylic sealer.

Adding the Hardware

I created hardware for my lure using copper wire, but you can use commercially available hardware if you like. Instead of an elaborate copper loop system attached with wood screws, a simple screw eye will allow you to attach a hanging wire or fishing line.

further reading

Whittling Decorative Fishing Lures
By Lora S. Irish

This comprehensive forty-page booklet contains extended carving and painting instructions for the folk-art lure featured in this article, plus a total of nine fishing lure patterns, and instructions for making your own decorative hardware and display stand.

Available in two versions: printed for $12.95, and digital e-book for $9.99, from Fox Chapel Publishing, 1970 Broad St., East Petersburg, Pa., 17520, 800-457-9112, www.foxchapelpublishing.com.

further reading

Lure and Decoy Pattern Packs
By Lora S. Irish

Exclusive pattern sets available two ways: digital download or printed. Fishing Lure Patterns (code cp098p) contains thirty-eight patterns, and Ice-Fishing Decoy Patterns (code cp099p) contains eight large patterns.

Digital downloads are $12.95 each at Lora's website, www.carvingpatterns.com. Reference codes to order printed patterns for $12.95 from Fox Chapel Publishing, 1970 Broad St., East Petersburg, Pa., 17520, 800-457-9112, www.foxchapelpublishing.com.

For more information on Lora S. Irish, see page 96.

ONLINE BONUS
Download instructions for making a fishing lure display stand.
woodcarvingillustrated.com

MATERIALS:

- ⅞" x 1½" x 4" (22mm x 38mm x 102mm) basswood (lure)
- ⅛" x 1½" x 1¾" (3mm x 38mm x 44mm) basswood (tail)
- Scrap paper and cereal box cardboard (templates)
- Sandpaper: 220 grit
- Cyanoacrylate (CA) glue (such as Super Glue®) or wood glue
- Acrylic paints: black, titanium white, medium green, pale yellow, red, burnt sienna
- Permanent marking pens: metallic gold or silver (optional)
- Gloss spray acrylic sealer
- 2 each ¼" (6mm) wood screws

materials & tools

TOOLS:

- Knife
- Pencil with a new eraser
- Wire cutters (optional)
- Flat-nose pliers
- Craft scissors
- Penny (or use template)
- Brown paper bag
- Well-used toothbrush
- 18- or 12- gauge copper, colored copper, or aluminum wire (optional) (available as jewelry supplies)
- Paintbrushes
- Palette

The author used these products for the project. Substitute your choice of brands, tools, and materials as desired.

Fish lure pattern

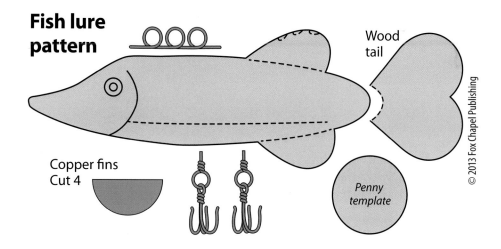

Wood tail

Copper fins
Cut 4

Penny template

© 2013 Fox Chapel Publishing

Make the chore of sorting through mail a bit more tolerable with this twig-carved letter opener. It also makes a great gift for any dad or grad.

Letter Opener

Four simple steps to a long-lasting tool

By Chris Lubkemann

A letter opener is just a wooden knife intended for use opening envelopes. It can be of almost any size and be carved from either a branch or a piece of straight-grained milled wood. Before long, you'll be slitting open envelopes with style!

1 Choose a straight branch that is free of knots. If the branch has a slight curve, make sure that when you carve the blade, you end up with a blade that is straight when you look at it from the top. Seeing the curve of the branch from the side is fine. If there is any knot on the branch, it should be either at the butt end of the handle or at the spot where the handle transitions to the blade.

2 With your knife, flatten both sides of the branch to make the blade, leaving the handle portion round.

3 Finish shaping the blade, notching the division between the handle and the blade.

4 With fine grit sandpaper, smooth and sharpen the blade. Finish the opener as desired. All kinds of variations can be done with the handle, both in terms of the carving itself and in the burning and decoration.

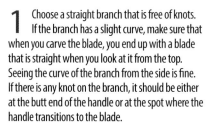

materials & tools

MATERIALS:
- Straight branch, free of knots

TOOLS:
- Pocketknife
- Fine grit sandpaper
- Woodburner (optional)

The author used these products for the project.
Substitute your choice of brands, tools, and materials as desired.

Carve a
Caricature
Pig

Charming character makes an ideal beginner project

By Christine Coffman

This little porker is big on personality, but can be completed with just a few basic tools. Beginners can expect good results with their first attempt, and more experienced carvers can fill a pig pen in a weekend.

I prefer the Warren #8B and #20EX blades. The #8B is slightly curved and the #20EX is sharpened on the outside curve of the blade. The #20EX is great for making cuts on a flat surface. I also use a Drake knife with the blade mounted at an angle toward the handle. This design creates very little stress on the wrist.

Whatever tools you choose, make sure they are sharp. Sharp tools require less pressure to make the cut, which gives you more control and smoother cuts. Anytime you work with sharp tools, protect your thumb with a thumb guard. Pay attention to what will happen if your knife slips and keep all parts of your hand out of that potential path.

Transfer the pattern onto the blank. Make sure the grain runs parallel with the pig's legs. Many boards check or crack at the ends because the exposed end grain dries faster. Position your pattern away from the end of the board.

PIG: ROUGHING OUT

1 **Cut the profile.** Use a band saw or a coping saw. Cut away any sharp angles. Clamp the pig in a vise and use a hand saw to make a cut separating the two front legs and the two back legs. Do not cut too deep in the belly area. Sand the bottom of the feet smooth and level.

2 **Rough out the body.** For greater control, cut thin slices of wood away from the carving. Round the pig's body. Leave extra wood for the tail. Carve all of the areas equally. Don't spend too much time carving in one spot. Block in the tail and continue rounding the body.

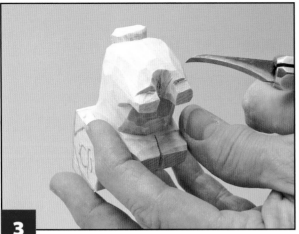

TIPS SMOOTH CUTS

If you feel resistance as you make the cut or notice the cut is leaving a rough surface, change the direction of your cut or sharpen your blade.

3 **Define the legs.** Use the tip of a knife to make a stop cut along the area you want to remain. Repeat this step to make a slight groove. Carve up to the stop cut, making small cuts to avoid snapping off the legs. Thin the legs and feet.

PIG: ADDING DEFINITION

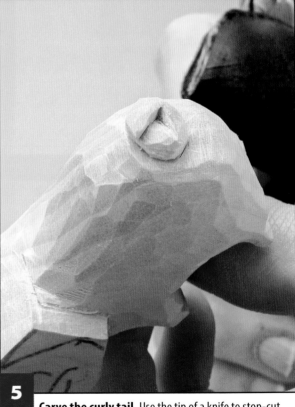

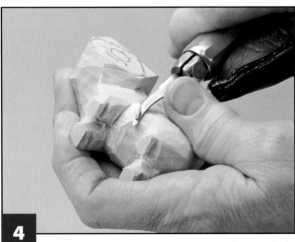

4 **Refine the overall shape.** Remove wood from the back of the head. Use stop cuts and thin slicing cuts to define the upper part of the legs and round the belly. Keep turning the figure and carve all of the areas equally.

5 **Carve the curly tail.** Use the tip of a knife to stop-cut along the area where the tail overlaps itself. Cut down into the center of the tail to make it look like a doughnut. Separate the tail where it overlaps, clean up the cuts, and smooth the surface of the tail.

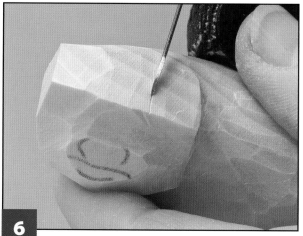

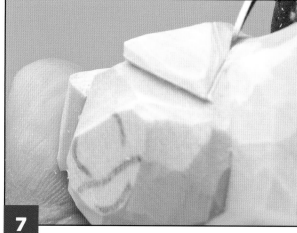

6   **Rough out the pig's face.** Carve away the wood from the sides of the pig's face. Leave wood for the snout. Stop-cut around the edge of the ears on top of the head with the tip of the knife. Begin removing the waste wood between the ears.

7   **Finish carving the ears.** Stop-cut around the front and sides of the ears, giving them a triangular shape. Relieve the wood around the ears. A curved blade with the outside edge sharpened, such as a Warren #20EX, is useful for this step.

PIG: CARVING THE DETAILS

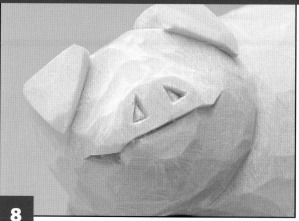

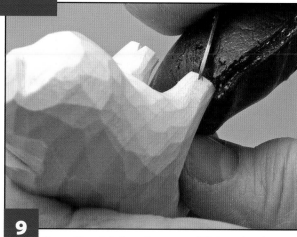

8   **Carve the mouth and snout.** Make a stop cut along the upper jaw line and carve up to this line from below to make the chin smaller than the snout. Smooth and shape the chin and snout. Stop-cut around the triangular nostrils and carve away the wood inside the nostrils.

9   **Carve the pig's feet.** Carve a small V-shaped wedge from the front of the pig's feet to simulate cloven hooves.

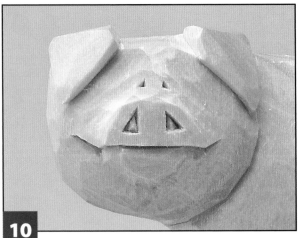

10 **Finish the carving.** Carve two tiny triangular eyes set close together. Go over the entire carving and remove any rough cuts. Use a knife to add your signature and the date.

11 **Apply the finish.** Dip the carving in Formby's low-gloss tung oil. Wipe off the excess and let it dry overnight. Dip the carving again and let it dry overnight.

Caricature pig patterns

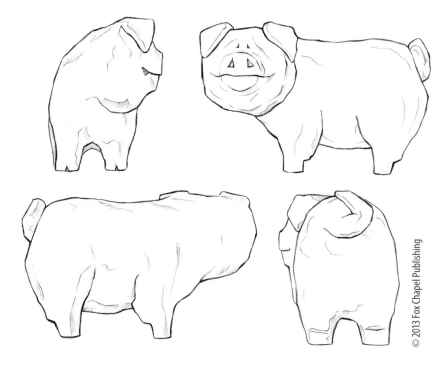

© 2013 Fox Chapel Publishing

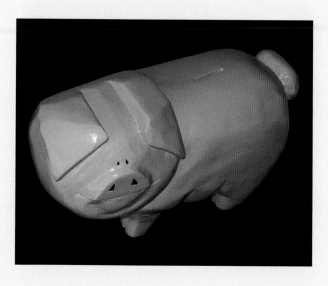

Piggy Bank

Michael Carroll of Hampton Falls, N.H., created a piggy bank for his infant granddaughter using Christine Coffman's caricature pig pattern. Michael enlarged the pig slightly and hollowed the inside to turn the carving into a bank.

For more information on Christine Coffman, see page 96.

Slingshot

Get into trouble with this toy for all ages

By Chris Lubkemann

My interest in slingshots came very naturally, as it also did with bows and arrows, different kinds of traps, tree houses, and peashooters (except we made little clay balls to shoot in our nice, straight bamboo barrels). Though I'm not proud of all of the things I did as a kid with my many slingshots, I did do a lot of fun and useful things, too—like pick way-out-on-a-limb, impossible-to-reach mangoes!

Of course it was a two-person job. One stood under the huge, beautiful, ripe mango, and the other stood off a ways armed with a nice, hard green guava or palm nut and a good slingshot. The idea, naturally, was not to hit the mango itself. That would bruise it unmercifully. The actual target was the long stem just above the mango. This being clipped by the speeding "bullet," the mango would come straight down, into the hands (hopefully) of the waiting catcher.

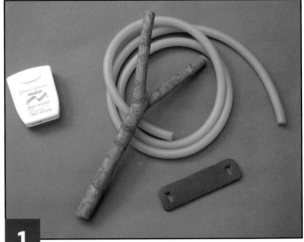

1 The components for a 2005 Lubkemann adaptation of a 1950s Brazilian slingshot, Mato Grosso style: a hardwood fork in a reasonably symmetrical Y; good-quality surgical tubing (how thick depends on how strong a pull you want); a good piece of leather for the pocket; and dental floss (yes, dental floss!—it can be mint-flavored or plain, and I generally use waxed). It's very strong and doesn't slip when you're tying it.

2 Cut the handle branch to a length you feel comfortable with.

3 Round off the tops of the two top stems of the fork.

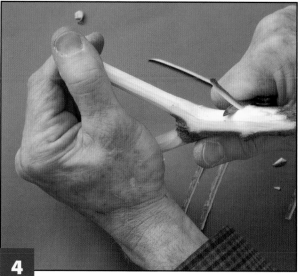

4 For this particular fork, we'll strip all of the bark off. For some of my slingshot forks, I leave on part of the bark, depending on what I want the final fork to look like.

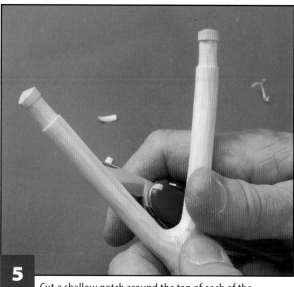

5 Cut a shallow notch around the top of each of the rubber-holding branches.

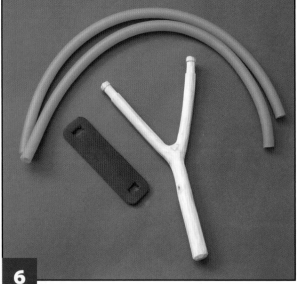

6 Cut the tubing to the length you want, remembering that you're going to fold the ends around the shallow notches in the two top stems and through the holes you've carefully cut in the piece of leather. When you cut the holes in the leather pouch, make sure you cut very carefully so as not to overcut, thus leaving little cuts that can develop into rips or tears in the leather.

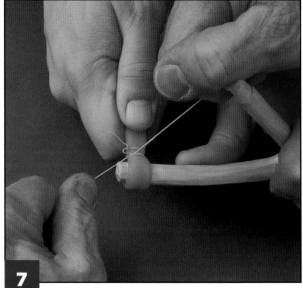

7 Tying the rubber to the fork is definitely a two-person job! One person holds the fork and stretches the rubber (with the tab on the outside of the fork), and the other person wraps the floss tightly around the stretched rubber tubing and ties it. Don't spare the floss! Double it and use lots. And tie several knots as you go along the wrapping and tying process.

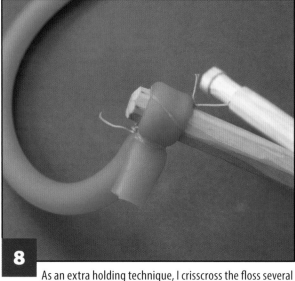

8 As an extra holding technique, I crisscross the floss several times across the front of the rubber and around the notched stem of the fork.

materials
& tools

MATERIALS:
- Hardwood fork in a reasonably symmetrical Y
- Good-quality surgical tubing
- Leather for the pocket
- Dental floss

TOOLS:
- Pocketknife
- Sandpaper—a couple of grits on the fine to very fine side (150- and 220-grit would work).

The author used these products for the project.
Substitute your choice of brands, tools, and materials as desired.

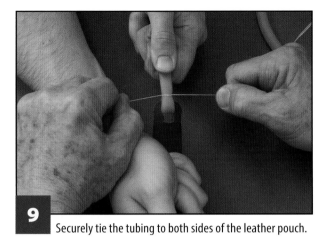

9 Securely tie the tubing to both sides of the leather pouch.

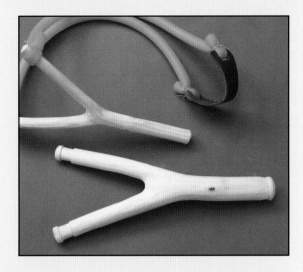

The particular fork that we used to make this slingshot, while of strong wood, is probably a bit thinner than I would normally use for this heavier gauge surgical tubing. The thicker fork at the bottom would be a better choice.

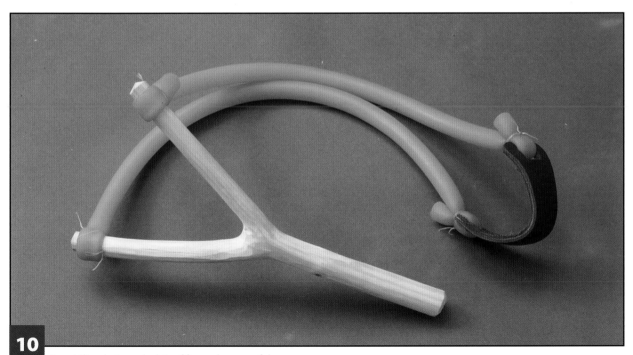

10 Done! Slingshots can be lots of fun and very useful, when they're used right. Some states may have special laws and regulations relating to slingshots. Be sure to check before putting yours to use. 'Nuff said!

Form and function define this
attractive wall hook. Make several
and hang them wherever you notice
clutter around the house.

Wall Hooks

Bring the outdoors into your home

By Chris Lubkemann

These hook branches are mounted on a backerboard fastened to a wall or door. These little guys are quite convenient to have in those places where you just need to hang something up—next to the kitchen sink for that damp dishcloth, perhaps? Or next to your bed, where you always forget to put your belt or favorite necklace someplace where you can find it in the morning? The list goes on...

materials & tools

MATERIALS:
- Sturdy branch
- Milled lumber for backerboard
- Carpenter's glue

TOOLS:
- Handsaw
- Pocketknife
- Sandpaper
- Handheld power drill
- Bit for pilot holes to match screws
- Screws

The author used these products for the project. Substitute your choice of brands, tools, and materials as desired.

1 Choose your coat hook branches and various sized pieces of milled lumber for backerboards.

2 Trim the hook branches to the sizes you want and round all the ends of the branches. If you want to have a light-colored coat hook, remove all the bark and sand the branch smooth.

3 Cut the base of the branch according to the angle at which you want to attach the hook to its backerboard.

4 Attach the branch to the backerboard. Drill a pilot hole first, then screw in from the back of the board. For a little more strength, you might want to use a bit of carpenter's glue, too.

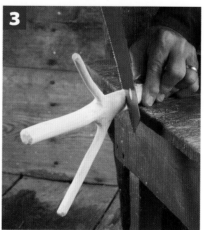

Use some straight branch sections and a longer backerboard to make a peg rack.

A small hook is perfect for keys or jewelry.

Mix dark hooks with light backerboards for some extra pop.

A single Y branch is yet another choice when creating hooks.

Name Pins

Great, personalized gifts

By Chris Lubkemann

Select branches that are about 5/16–1/2" (10–15mm) in diameter and cut them into 2–3" (50–75mm)-long pieces. That way, your pins will always be just the right size. This is a great project to do with kids. You can put them in charge of decorating the pins as you carve more, or you can ask them to glue on the pin backs. They'll be thrilled when they get to wear and show off the finished product.

materials & tools

MATERIALS:

- Several branches about 5/16–1/2" (10–15mm) thick
- Heavy block or board

TOOLS:

- Knife
- Sandpaper
- Handsaw or pull saw
- Pin backs
- Wood glue
- Woodburner
- Colored permanent markers (optional)

The author used these products for the project. Substitute your choice of brands, tools, and materials as desired.

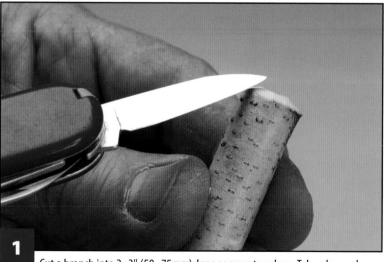

1 Cut a branch into 2–3" (50–75mm)-long segments or logs. Take a log and round both ends with your knife.

2 Split the log by placing it upright and positioning your knife across the center of the top. Use a board or heavy block to strike the knife and drive it into the log like an ax. One or two good hits should split the log in half.

3 Smooth the flat side of each half of the log with your knife.

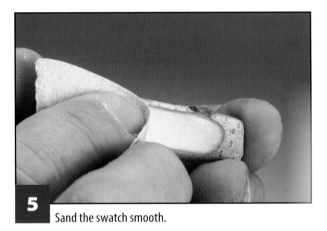

4 Flip the pieces over and cut a swatch on the round side of the pin, cutting from each end toward the middle.

5 Sand the swatch smooth.

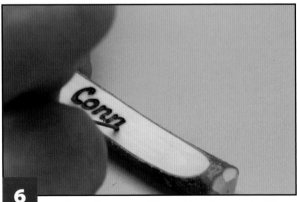

6 Woodburn the name and design(s) on the swatch. Color the drawings with permanent markers if you want the log to be a bit brighter. Natural shading with the woodburner also looks nice; it all depends on your taste.

7 Using carpenter's wood glue, glue a pin back on the flat side of your log.

Fences for Everything

From large to small, every size fence has its uses

By Chris Lubkemann

Fences are great outside for keeping pesky animals away from your garden or for preventing your dog from visiting your neighbor's tree. Since they're so useful outside, why not make an indoor fence that's just as useful? These miniature fences can be scaled up or down as needed and have all kinds of useful and decorative applications. Use them as letter holders, napkin holders, or settings for whittled roosters. You can make personalized ones for your kids to hold school papers or homework. See what other uses you can come up with for this versatile project.

materials & tools

MATERIALS:
- Scrap milled blocks for the base
- Branches for the fence posts
- Thin branches for fence rails

TOOLS:
- Knife
- Drill and bits
- Handsaw or Japanese pull saw
- Awl or nail
- Wood glue

The author used these products for the project. Substitute your choice of brands, tools, and materials as desired.

1 Make your base block, and use the drill to "dig" the holes for the fence posts. (I'm using a Forstner bit here.)

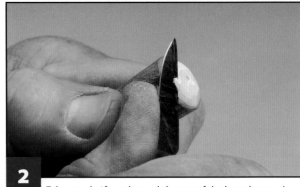

2 Take your knife and round the top of the branches you're using as your fence posts.

3 Use your saw and knife to narrow the bottom of each fencepost to match the diameter of the holes you drilled in the base block. Doing this allows the bottom of the fence post to overlap the hole slightly. It will probably look better this way than if you stick the post straight into the hole, especially if the fence post is not exactly round.

4 Using an awl (or nail), mark the locations on each fence post where you'll drill holes for the fence rails.

5 Drill the holes for the rails. (Drilling a dry, seasoned branch will produce a much cleaner hole than a green branch.)

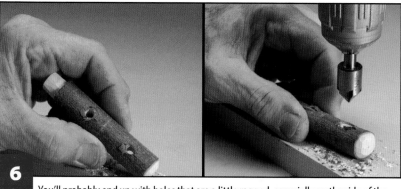

6 You'll probably end up with holes that are a little ragged, especially on the side of the post where the drill bit exits. Clean out the edges of the hole with a countersink bit, or clean off the rough edges with the tip of your pocketknife. If you use the pocketknife method, be careful to cut in a direction that allows you to keep as much bark as you want.

7 Insert the fenceposts into the base block and the rails into the posts, using a bit of wood glue to keep the fence tight.

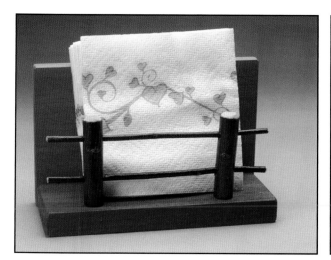

As shown by the photos, you can use your mini fence any way you want: as a napkin holder, letter holder, recipe or business card holder.

Contributors

The child of missionaries, Chris Lubkemann grew up in the forests of Brazil and Peru, and has been carving since age seven. His smallest whittling — a branch rooster — was given a Guinness World Record Certificate in 1981. He lives in Lancaster, Pa., and demonstrates at the Amish Farm and House. Visit Chris at www.WhittlingWithChris.com.

Rick Wiebe lives in Westbank, B.C., Canada, and has been teaching woodcarving since 1987. He runs Wood 'N Wildcraft, has self-published two instructional carving books, and can be found at www.woodcarvingbiz.com.

Ron Johnson lives in Mobile, Ala., belongs to the Delta Woodcarvers of Mobile and has been a member of the National Woodcarving Association since 1972. Contact Ron at robojo222@yahoo.com to talk whittling and exchange Santa pencils.

Jan Oegema lives in Bowmanville, Ont., Canada. Visit Jan at www.janscarvingstudio.com or check out his woodspirit study stick at www.foxchapelpublishing.com.

Kivel Weaver of Fayetteville, Ark., has carved more chains than he can count with his modified Case pocketknife. Check out his amazing chains at www.woodcarvingillustrated.com/techniques/hand-carved-classics.html.

Tom Hindes, retired from a career at Ohio State University, picked up a whittling knife six years ago and now carves Noah's arks, Christmas ornaments, wizards, and gnomes.

Carol Kent of Jackson, Mich., started carving at a Boy Scout Jamboree and hasn't quit. Her work has earned best of show and people's choice awards at woodcarving and art shows

Addison "Dusty" Dussinger, of Lancaster, Pa., is a founding member of the Lancaster County Woodcarvers. He teaches classes, has been featured on television, and has received the prestigious Ed Harrington Award.

Everett Ellenwood is the author of The Complete Book of Woodcarving (Fox Chapel Publishing) and the producer of popular carving and sharpening DVDs. Visit Everett at www.ellenwoodarts.com.

Kathleen Schuck began carving in 1950 and owned a carving store for eighteen years. A BSA Carving Merit Badge counselor, she continues to teach and has twice received a teaching grant for children from The International Wildfowl Carvers Association.

A prolific designer and carver, Lora S. Irish is the author of several woodcarving books that can be found at www.FoxChapelPublishing.com. Visit Lora's enormous warehouse of digital carving patterns at www.carvingpatterns.com.

Christine Coffman lives in Rochester, Wash and has been carving her own patterns since she was twelve years old. Visit her at www.christmas-carvings.com.